D0016574

More Praise for <u>The StreetWise Investor</u>

"Charles Fahy and Sydney LeBlanc offer important insight into Wall Street in layman's terms. Required reading for everyone who bought on a "hot" tip and paid the price for doing so. Charles' long-term investment philosophy is critical to investment success."

Charles H. Brandes
President
Brandes Investment Management, Inc.

"*The StreetWise Investor* makes a single, basic point and illustrates it in various helpful ways. In short, excellent material well presented!"

Enno Hobbing
National Association of Securities Dealers, Inc.

"What a book! *The StreetWise Investor* is a fun, fast read, filled with common sense and sound practical advice. This Texan stockbroker, Charles Fahy, is the Will Rogers of Wall Street!"

Gary Meyers
Syndicated Columnist

"In any endeavor, there are positives and negatives to deal with. Having the knowledge to differentiate the two is key to success. It would take anyone twenty years of trial-and-error investing to gain the knowledge available in this book."

Daniel Bott, CIMC
Chairman, Advisory Board and
Co-Founder, Institute for Investment Management Consultants

THE STREETWISE INVESTOR

CHARLES L. FAHY
WITH SYDNEY LeBLANC

PROBUS PUBLISHING COMPANY
Chicago, Illinois
Cambridge, England

© 1993, Probus Publishing Company

ALL RIGHTS RESERVED. No part of this publication may be reproduced, stored in a retrieval system, or transmitted by any means, electronic, mechanical, photocopying, recording, or otherwise, without the prior written permission of the publisher and the copyright holder.

This publication is designed to provide accurate and authoritative information in regard to the subject matter covered. It is sold with the understanding that the publisher is not engaged in rendering legal, accounting or other professional service.

Authorization to photocopy items for internal or personal use, or the internal or personal use of specific clients, is granted by PROBUS PUBLISHING COMPANY, provided that the US$7.00 per page fee is paid directly to Copyright Clearance Center, 27 Congress Street, Salem MA 01970, USA. For those organizations that have been granted a photocopy license by CCC, a separate system of payment has been arranged. The fee code for users of the Transactional Reporting Service is: 1-55738-445-2/93/$0.00 + $7.00.

ISBN 1-55738-445-2

Printed in the United States of America

BB

1   2   3   4   5   6   7   8   9   0

This book is dedicated to all of my clients and JJF, who taught me.

—Charles Fahy

Table of Contents

Don't Tell Me How to Invest! Just Tell Me Which Stocks Are Going Up!

What? *Another* book about Wall Street?
It's just what you *don't* need, right?

Well, yes and no.

First, let me tell you what you *don't* need.

You don't need charts, statistics and other technical data to help you beat the system. You don't need trading secrets from Wall Street gurus. You don't need marketing hype about the latest high-yield, no-risk investment products. And you certainly don't need another jargon-filled volume of nonsense designed to confuse or intimidate you into buying something you don't understand.

Simply put, the reason you *do* need this book is to discover the answer to this puzzling question: *Why is it if the stock market works 100 percent of the time, that 80 percent of the time the investors' portfolios fail to perform?*

Picture this scenario: You buy a stock. What does it do? Right! It goes down. You ride it all the way south, get fed up, then sell it. What happens then?

Right again! It goes up!

If your head is bobbing up and down in agreement, then I'm talking to you and the other 79 percent who deserve a straight answer to a question that plagues millions of investors all over the world: *If history proves that the stock market works, why won't it work for me?*

The answer is simple and can be answered in three words.

And I'll talk about those three words and more in the following chapters so you'll have a full and clear understanding of how Wall Street really operates.

Together, we'll strip away the layers of illusion that surround Wall Street which make it impossible for you to make informed decisions. This book will expose marketing gimmicks of the business and how the industry plays to human nature until you allow yourself to be conned into making inappropriate investments.

The investment business is unnecessarily shrouded in mystery—a deliberate distraction wrapped around a sales pitch. The pundits on Wall Street would like you to believe that the world of securities is so big and complicated no one can understand all of its complexities. This is a lot of bull.

I've been in this business since 1972 and it took a few of my rookie years to grasp a true understanding of how the investment world revolves around us, and to figure out how I could accurately teach my clients about the realities of investing—*minus the sales jargon!* Being a logical person, I questioned many of the "absolutes" that were handed down to me. And because of my relentless pursuit of the truth about this business, the answers unfolded and I was able to change my business and my life.

Now, don't get me wrong. I love this business and the satisfaction it has given me all these years. I deeply respect my fellow brokers who strive to maintain honesty and integrity in their businesses. I admire the firms that are slowly changing their "sell the sizzle" attitude to a more compassionate, educational method of attracting and retaining customers.

Unfortunately, all it takes is a few bad actors giving poor performances to generate years of bad reviews for an entire profession to live down. As most of you know, the securities industry is one of the most highly regulated and tightly governed businesses in the world. With billions of dollars worth of capital passing through thousands of human hands, computers and sophisticated trading systems, we can feel fairly safe that our investment transactions are being properly watched and executed. This whole speedy process can make you dizzy.

But what you, the individual investor, need to concentrate on is *learning to distinguish between a good investment and a bad investment.* I will teach you, through this book, how to watch for the red flags, how to tear apart an investment using a few simple rules, how to recognize the difference between a professional investment counselor and a stock jockey, and how to separate truth from hype.

Most important, I will take you through the most critical process of all, by which the majority of decisions are made, fortunes gained or lost, lives enriched or unrewarded—*human nature*—the pulse of the stock market.

Between the pages of this book, I will do my best to share with you the valuable lessons I've learned, help you avoid the kinds of mistakes I've made during my career, teach you the secrets Wall Street keeps from you, and guide you to a better understanding of the psychology of the marketplace.

What I hope to accomplish with the information contained in this book is that you will come to understand me and my methods and the stock market as well as I have come to understand you, the investor, and the undeniable force of human nature.

Heaven or Hell?

Before we begin, I'd like to kick off the book with a joke a colleague of mine passed on to me recently. My reaction was one of "good new/ bad news." The good news was I loved the joke. The bad news was it really hit a chord with me and prompted me to undertake two years and two hundred pages of writing to complete this book. You'll see how this particular joke rings true through most of the book! When you finish the book, see if you agree with me.

A stockbroker died and found himself standing before the gates of Heaven with St. Peter. St. Peter told the stockbroker that he had been very religious and had always made the right decisions when faced with tough choices.

"Now, my son, you have just one more decision to make," said St. Peter. "Where do you wish to spend eternity—in Heaven or Hell?"

The stockbroker was puzzled as to why he'd be asked such an obvious question. But then, he reverted to his normal method of decision making. "Can I do a little research?" he said. "You know. Maybe spend a couple minutes in Heaven and a couple minutes in Hell before making up my mind."

St. Peter seemed surprised, but replied, "As you wish, my son."

The stockbroker then walked though the pearly gates. Inside, he found a place of indescribable beauty and unbelievable serenity where all men lived as brothers. He was so deeply moved that he cried.

The stockbroker returned to St. Peter. "I never knew such bliss was possible," he said as he wiped away his tears.

"You've made a wise decision, my son," said St. Peter.

The stockbroker hesitated for a moment, then said, "You don't suppose that maybe I could see what Hell is like? I mean, just out of curiosity?"

"Certainly, my son," said St. Peter. With the snap of a finger, the stockbroker was in Hell. To his astonishment, everyone was having a great time. If you played golf, every shot went 2,000 yards for a hole in one. If you played poker, you got five aces every hand.

The stockbroker couldn't wait to get back to St. Peter. "Heaven was nice," said the stockbroker. "But I just *have* to go to Hell!"

St. Peter scowled, but said, "As you wish, my son." And with the snap of a finger, the stockbroker was back in Hell. Only this time, Hell was filled with fire and smoke and the sounds of lost souls screaming in agony. The stockbroker suddenly felt a presence beside him. He turned and saw it was none other than Satan himself.

"What's going on?" shouted the stockbroker.

"Whatever do you mean?" said Satan, with mock innocence.

"Why, I was here just a few moments ago and it was fun!" screamed the stockbroker. "Everyone was having a great time! What happened?"

"It's simple," said Satan. "A few moments ago, you were a prospect; now you're a client!"

As we come to realize how rare it is to deal with honest and straightforward business people, the more we will be able to appreciate this anecdote. The chapters that follow will brighten the way for you.

Acknowledgments

The experience of writing a book has once again reminded me of the value of the mind's energy: Without it, like so much in life, all fizzles.

I want to thank Sydney LeBlanc for the fuel provided to make the work possible. Thanks not only for her professional skills, but also for her personal enthusiasm, which kept the project in focus toward the goal. Her industry contacts are also a tribute to her professional capacities.

My wife, Janet, played unequaled roles of best business partner and wonderful mother, stashing the kids away to allow time for my writing. Sherry

Atkinson, my registered assistant, helped organize my main business and helped keep the book project in check. Countless exchanges of data made Sherry one of the world's foremost experts in the overnight delivery of packages and fax machine engineering. Sherry literally runs my daytime schedule and my wife runs my nighttime schedule.

The evolution of writing *The Streetwise Investor* came about as a result of writing for the *Fort Bend Lifestyle* magazine. I thank Bill and Linda Anderson for the opportunity they provided me.

I would also like to thank nationally syndicated columnist Gary Meyers of Chicago for using me as a news resource, which inspired me throughout the years. Last, but not least, a personal thanks to Larry Chambers, author of *First-Time Investor* and *Recondo*.

My learning process is a result of reading everything I can find, especially from the national magazines. I have tried to provide the best credits my memory and collection of articles provide me. If I missed someone, it is not intentional.

Edwinia Ion, thanks for being a catalyst in my writing career.

1

I Didn't Want to Be a "Street" Person

I *knew* I'd be a washout. Never in my wildest dreams could I have imagined being a successful stockbroker. I was a terrible accounting student. I would never pass the licensing exam! Looking back, I laugh when I think of how uninformed I was about the business.

I had one of my first tastes of the stock market when I was in the eighth grade. My dad had accumulated quite a bit of IBM stock while he was serving in the military. The market was roaring—back in the 40s and 50s—and stocks were flying high.

My family and I joked about how his moods were determined by the ticker tape. If I wanted an allowance raise, I made doggone sure IBM had gone up all week before I asked him. I remember reading the IBM quotes in the paper after school to make sure the market was on my side!

My second real taste of the market occurred when I was on medical hold in the army (me and my parachute disagreed as to when it was supposed to open—and I lost). I volunteered to do a certain job on base over the holidays and for that I received double pay, which totaled about $2,000. That was quite a bit of money back then.

So, now I'm rich, I thought. I found a broker I liked by the name of Jack Daniels (!) and he recommended a mutual fund, while I came up with a stock I liked. I put $1,000 in each investment. Shortly thereafter, I received my orders to go overseas.

Well, about a year-and-a-half passed and when I got a chance to check my portfolio, to my surprise my $2,000 investment had grown to a whopping $5,000! *I thought I was a dang genius.* My broker was probably chuckling because he knew that anything you put into the market (back in 1970-72) shot sky high. It's what I call the "Rip van Winkle Effect." I was out of touch for two whole years and the market went up in spite of my absence!

Nonetheless, I was impressed with myself and my new-found fortune.

Wall Street Training 101

I didn't know it at the time, but during college when I was busy selling waterless cookware, encyclopedias, insurance and yes, even Bibles, I was preparing for my entree into the ever-changing world of Wall Street.

After college, I moved to the East Coast, figuring the job market was better in New York than in Georgia (where I had some roots). After running up and down Garden State Parkway for weeks on end without a lead, I decided to see a headhunter.

"So now I'm rich, I thought."

"You're an excellent salesman, and very persistent, too," said the headhunter. "Why don't you try a career on Wall Street as a stockbroker?"

"I flunked accounting. Wall Street wouldn't have any use for me," I said. (I felt I was good at making money; I would leave the accounting to someone else.)

"Heavens, you don't need to know a thing about accounting," laughed the headhunter. "The analysts take care of that end of things. All you need is a desk and a phone. You're a likable guy and you seem real personable. I think you'd be great!"

I told him that I had "dabbled" in the market and that was all he needed to send me on to EF Hutton, Merrill Lynch and Harris & Upham for interviews. After all was said and done, Hutton never responded, Merrill told me I wouldn't make a good salesman and I heard Harris & Upham were having back room trouble. I didn't know what that meant—

whether they were having affairs or what back there! (I found out later this meant operational difficulties.)

Later, persistence paid off with Hutton because that's where I found my training ground. Now, I still was not convinced I was cut out to be a Wall Street type. I had failed every test I had to take—or at best managed to get a C—because I'm just not a good test-taker. But, I had a wife, two kids and two weeks left on my unemployment, so I needed something *fast*.

My attitude was that I could learn about stocks, get $800 a month and look for a "real" job when I was supposed to be out looking for new clients.

Well, training by making 100 telephone cold calls per day left little time searching for greener pastures, I quickly learned. Plus, I grew tired of the four-hour commute every day. So as impetuous as I was, before I was even a registered broker, I asked for a transfer my last month in training, which landed me smack in the middle of Houston in December of 1972.

I finally became a broker in February of 1973. The Dow Jones had reached a new high of just over 1000 at that point and, as fate would have it, proceeded to go downhill that very day until the middle of 1974. So much for a celebration.

Dialing for Dollars

The market was a real bear, and of the 22 brokers I joined in '72, only two of us remained at the bottom of the market in '74. I guess you could say my persistence paid off once again, because like a dummy, I was still making 100 cold calls a day. In those days, the firm told me if I dialed 100 phone numbers I'd get rich. To me, there was no reason to presume that that statement was just a figure of speech. So, that's what I did. And it worked. And the more it worked, the more I kept dialing.

Let me explain the numbers game in the brokerage business. It's no different than if you're selling a product in a department store and 100 potential customers walk by your product. Out of the 100 people, 10 to 15 of them will stop. Out of the 10 to 15 that stop, two or three will buy. For a stockbroker, for every 100 people called, two or three will become clients. Instead of cold calling for clients, a broker might have a seminar where 10 to 15 people show up. That's the equivalent of cold calling 100 people. And that's how I began to build my business.

Make the Clients Happy . . . at Their Cost?

The next two years yielded a very strong upturn in the market and the bull was roaring once again. I was doing a very good job of building my business. However, a vague feeling of dissatisfaction kept creeping over me, an uneasiness I couldn't quite put my finger on. What was happening to me was that I was beginning to realize some of the fallacies of this business.

As exciting as it was getting launched in the business, experimenting with marketing and working the numbers game, I started to notice a problem: *The more clients I obtained, the less time I had to market or prospect for others.* I was getting to the point to where I had no time to research my investment ideas. Not to mention that servicing my clients was getting a little thin. I was in the middle of a dilemma.

I also noticed that many times I placated my clients by doing what *they* wanted to do in the market. At 25 years of age, I made the assumption that if my client was older than I was, he had to know more than I did. And he certainly had more money, so my inclination was to listen to the client and whatever made the client happy, made me happy. That was the name of the game. My motto was "make a customer happy, qualify his investment preferences, sell him the product and make a commission." And, Lord knows, I did that well. I burned up the track record for sales with my "keep 'em happy" attitude.

Soon, though, that vague feeling of uneasiness hit me right between the eyes. After some careful calculations and reviews of account sheets, I noticed, to my dismay that, after two years in a row of a bull market, very few of my customers were making money. Something was screwy. My investments weren't working! But that was only part of the dismal equation.

Now I began to understand why the firm kept telling us that we would probably lose 70 percent of our customers and that's why we had to keep prospecting. Well, no one ever bothered to explain *why* the attrition rate was so high. When I finally figured out the most obvious answer, I felt as though I had been hit on the head with a two-by-four. And that's when my business really started to change.

I'll Tell the Pilot How to Fly!

Before I launch into that important revelation, let me say a bit more about client attrition. An example: A hypothetical client is with a broker for a year or a year-and-a-half. He'll make ten trades, trades that he instructed the broker to execute. Eight of them will be profitable and two of them will be losses. It was fun for the client and the broker made a good commission. But take a close look at the transaction: The client probably made eight one-point profits and two 10-point losses. Human nature being what it is, the client could go home and tell his wife, "Honey, we just made another profit. That's the eighth one this year. And we've only had two losses." Well, it doesn't take a rocket scientist to figure out that it should be the other way around.

> **" burned up the track record for sales with my 'keep 'em happy' attitude."**

Soon the client tires of waiting for the profit turn-around and suddenly the broker becomes the scapegoat, even though the client directed the trades. The client accuses the broker of making all of the money. Now, think about it for a minute. Is the client right? Of course he is.

Some brokers are guilty of allowing clients to be the decision makers in the investment arena. That's what I term having the "passenger tell the airline pilot how to fly the plane."

In the beginning, many of my clients would ask for municipals. I knew mathematically that they'd be better off compounding in an annuity, for example, (even after taxes) than they would be in tax-exempts. I would always do what they wanted, because I was so eager to please, but I always started my sentences with, "I'll get you the bonds, but . . ." Then, like clockwork, a year or so later they would come back in and ask what they should do with the bonds *I* sold them. I would say in the nicest way I could, "I see in my notes that I warned you might have a loss on these bonds, that it would be better to put your money into an annuity." The point here is that I'd done everything right, and my customers would recognize that the product purchase was their idea, but I still lost in the end. Even though I'd sold a product my client wanted, with full disclosure, my clients still owned a lousy investment, and relationships built on these sorts of investments eventually soured.

> **"I** am not trying to win a popularity contest. My only job is to show my clients how to obtain the best performance from their portfolio."

As my business evolved and I saw the mistakes I made along the way with clients, my question to clients became, "If you agree with me and trust my system of investing, leave the decision making to me. If you like it, buy it. If not, leave it on the rack. Don't ask me to take it off the rack, shorten it, put purple stripes on it—because I won't do it." Not after all the lessons I've learned.

I was not trying to win a popularity contest. My only job was (and still is) to show my clients how to obtain the best performance from their portfolio—and, as a result, this technique will make me popular!

Investment Portfolios: R.I.P.

Attrition rate, or (figurative) death of an investor, occurs when a client loses money. And a client loses money when he doesn't fully understand the guts of an investment, when he gives in to human nature, or when he thinks he knows more than the dedicated, professional investment counselor.

Investors need to know some elementary facts about the market and they need to be open and willing to learn about their investments along the way. If not, they have no business in the marketplace.

Attrition also occurs when the broker gives in to the client and gets sucked in by all the marketing hype on a "fail-safe" investment. They both fall prey to what I call the "sales slick syndrome." This is a slick, four-color brochure that features an American flag, a bald eagle, green trees and oil wells gushing away on the cover. Ignore the splash and read the fine print in the accompanying prospectus. Make sure the broker explains the historical performance and the risk factors involved. There are many intelligent ways of examining investments, but before I put them on the table, I'll share with you how I spent my first ten years on Wall Street learning what *not* to do and why I can speak with so much compassion and authority on who and what doesn't work in the stock market.

2

The Investment Planning Puzzle: Putting the Pieces Together

There's a controlled madness to this business. I was slowly finding out that there was more to the investment equation than I had been taught. It was evident in many ways: client turnover, insufficient performance of portfolios, and unhappy investors. And even though these factors were driven home to me on an almost daily basis, I continued to sell the hot properties, the proprietary products, or the "stocks of the day" the firms would urge us to promote.

Pieces of the investment planning puzzle started falling into place for me around 1980 and I began to doubt the integrity of my own profession. Fortunately, I entered the age of "financial enlightenment" soon thereafter. I guess you could call it the end of an old career and the beginning of a new one. But before I tell you my story of how I catapulted myself and my clients to financial success, allow me to sprinkle this chapter with another equation: the tale of how $1 + 1 = 3$.

A Team Spirit— Good for Our Clients

Rookie broker John Phillips was the only other broker in the office who could give me a run for my money. He was a workaholic. We used to run circles around each other trying to outdo sales records, or production figures as we call them. But since we liked and respected each other, we didn't become arch rivals.

Some months John would get a big kick out of congratulating me for beating him in obtaining new accounts. And some months I would go over to his desk and shake his hand for getting a sales achievement award.

It soon dawned on both of us that instead of creating a competitive relationship, our interaction brought two high achievers together in a friendly, pleasant way. I wish I could say we were two brilliant brokers putting together a brilliant business merger, but in reality it was a relationship of fate, born of necessity. I was a bachelor father of three small children at the time and if I had important matters to tend to on behalf of the kids, or if they were sick, John would cover for me and take care of my clients. I would do the same for him when he was away from the office.

I noticed John had a deep concern for his clients. He was an astute investor and would put investors in money markets rather than in a product designed only to generate immediate commission revenue and eventually do poorly for them.

> **''Safety, preservation of capital, and performance became the key words.''**

I kept my eye on him and soon realized there was a common denominator between us—caring for clients. Now, I know this phrase seems to be a real buzzword today in the world of sales, but it wasn't so much of one a decade ago. After the market crash in 1987, investors were so skittish that service became the number one product. Investors and brokers alike were afraid to venture into anything that even hinted of risk. Tax-sheltered limited partnerships all but disappeared after the Tax Reform Act of 1986 (TRA'86) and many brokers found themselves revamping their businesses to include more insurance products, value stocks, and certificates of deposit. Many of the high-flying, super-hero brokers of the late 70s and early 80s found themselves either embroiled in bitter investor lawsuits or disappearing from the industry altogether.

Safety, preservation of capital, and performance became the key words and I quickly began to unlock the secrets of successful investing from their Wall Street hiding place to share them with my clients.

Everybody's Fired!

Back in the early days of our partnership, I made a startling discovery and immediately reported my findings to John. I walked into his office and said in a serious tone, "I've got some good news and some bad news for you. The good news is, I've finally figured out what we need to do so that we never, ever again have to worry about our clients losing money. From now on, we're going to make all kinds of money for their portfolios. We're going to make all kinds of commissions. We'll all be rich!"

Bewildered, John looked at me and said, "Well, if that's the good news, what could the bad news possibly be?"

"That's easy," I said. "You're fired."

Taken aback with my reply, he asked, "What do you mean?"

I told him not to worry because I was fired, too, and, for that matter, we were going to fire all of our customers.

John thought I had lost my mind. But, in reality, the lesson I learned during my first 10 years in business had finally surfaced: the two worst evils in running a portfolio were the stockbroker and the client.

Yes, the sinking logic of what was happening over and over in my business was beginning to make sense to me. The numbers game, the 70 percent attrition rate, the losing portfolios, the unhappy clients—all of these factors versus the fact that John and I were still burning up sales records and making a lot of money for ourselves made me take a hard look at the truth. And the truth was that the combination of human nature and investments that just don't work over the long haul was a deadly mix.

If It Looks and Smells Like Garbage—Don't Buy It!

No one really ever explained to my satisfaction the reasons for the high attrition rate I had learned about when I was in training. The answer is simply that some products are touted as being excellent investments and are nothing more than pre-packaged garbage. And selling junk will only produce more junk as a result. The losses from a poor investment wind up being dumped in the investor's lap, leaving him or her to deal with cleaning up the mess. This investor will eventually leave and search for another broker or leave the market entirely.

My logical mind said that if I sold investments that worked, I wouldn't lose 70 percent of my clients. My business would flourish, everyone would be happy. Seemed pretty straightforward to me.

If You Take Care of Business, It Will Take Care of You

So, I broke away from the traditional methods of doing business I learned years ago. I decided to spend more time with my clients to determine how to meet their needs, to determine which investments would work and would perform the best. My thoughts were that if I sold my clients what the firm urged me to sell or what they thought they wanted because they heard a hot stock tip or whatever, it wasn't going to work, so why bother? I would probably lose the client in a year anyway and I'd wind up being the bad guy for "recommending" a bad investment.

So from that day on, I focused on investments that worked and steered clear of anything and anybody that smelled like a bad deal. I made some incredible discoveries during that time and I'll reveal the details to you in the following chapters. But, let me continue with the rest of the story.

I decided to offer total financial planning and money management for clients and dubbed them the "file" clients. In the business, we have what are known as "position" sheets listing the investor's name, address, Social Security number, position of trades, buy/sell lists and so on. I went a step further and put an entire file together on my clients including copies of their tax returns, insurance policies, other investments, family information—everything I needed to thoroughly understand and plan for the client.

I wanted to acquire more "file" clients and less of what I call the "bookie" business. I felt I could work better if I could just change the way Wall Street operated in general! Taking on Wall Street machinery, however, proved to be more than I had anticipated.

Me and the "Bosses"

One afternoon, I met with one of the members of the board of directors for our firm and a regional sales vice president to outline my career game plan and solicit their help in my quest for a better way of doing business. I also asked for more administrative help as well as a new office layout with a design that permitted presentations on a chalkboard.

Well, to say I got myself into a lot of hot water that afternoon is an understatement. Being painfully honest, I put my feelings on the table and offered my 10 years of observations about the industry and how I hoped to effect a change in traditional sales methods. Bluntly, I said I felt we [brokers] were basically "selling machines" who didn't have the time to teach clients about the investment process. Then I offered my "ice cream analogy" and compared securities products to different flavors of ice cream. "The basic product stays the same; only the flavors change to entice the potential investor," I explained. I then referred to debt instruments as an example. I described it this way:

"You see, we'll take corporate bonds, change the name and they become unit trusts. Then we will call them closed-end funds or open-end funds, or package bonds. But bonds are bonds are bonds. They're a bad investment in my opinion. My point is that we have to stop selling investments as though they are bacon. Bacon smells good and sounds good frying in the pan, looks good on the breakfast plate and tastes delicious—but if we eat enough of it, it will kill us!"

> **"The two worst evils in running a portfolio were the stockbroker and the client."**

Well, if that wasn't enough to seal my coffin, the next phrase certainly did. "The truth is," I said, "we're selling junk to the American public!"

Then, I started in on what a joke tax-exempts were and, in a flash, the sales vice president jumped out of his chair and began wildly shaking his finger in my face.

"Charlie Fahy, you unappreciative young whipper-snapper," he shouted, his face turning a bright red. "How dare you have the audacity to come in here and accuse us of selling junk. My goodness gracious, when I hired you ten years ago, you were walking to work! Now, you're driving a Mercedes. You've been to Acapulco, Denmark, Bermuda on sales contest junkets. Why, you've been all over the world complements of this firm. Plus, you are earning over $100,000 a year to boot. How dare you come in here and tell us we sell junk to the American public right in front of one of the directors of our board!"

Acting relatively unaffected by this sudden verbal attack, I told the vice president that as one of the most senior veteran brokers, I get chewed out regularly in much the same manner by clients. And this makes for very unproductive days, not to mention the emotional upset and unhappy clients. I proceeded to explain in a very calm and logical manner the way in which I saw things. I pointed out again my business plan would double my commissions if the clients were satisfied. The clients would be better off, the company would be better off and I would be better off.

I said, "*You* don't buy the products I'm referring to for your personal account, do you? And you can bet *he* (pointing to the director) doesn't buy this stuff. When I get a bonus check each year for being a top producer, it goes right into a partnership award program—a capital account. In a bad year it makes a 10 percent return; in a good year, 30 percent. And, you both are doing the same with your own money— it's being professionally managed. You're not buying bonds or GNMAs!

I went on to explain how much more credibility we would all have if we could just take more time to teach our clients about risk versus reward, review their financial objectives, then invest and manage their portfolios the way we manage our own.

I was thinking how great it would be if I could tell my clients that I, and the firm, were investing our own money in the very same investments as they were. At this point, I felt confident. Who could argue this theory with me? I had them checkmated.

Shot Down

The director decided to speak up. He looked me square in the eye and asked, "Charlie, if you and your kids go to a fast food burger place and order hamburgers, french fries, and milk shakes, then when you start to pay for your order the person at the counter says he won't sell you the order because it's junk food—what would you do?"

He didn't wait for my answer. Instead, he quickly added, "You'd get mad and go over to another fast food restaurant, wouldn't you? Get with the program, Charlie. If we don't sell this stuff, the American public will buy it from a competitor."

With the analogy hanging in the air like a guilty verdict handed down by a jury, I was rendered speechless, and left the meeting.

I was discouraged, of course, but not defeated. I decided I would wait until another opportunity presented itself to discuss my proposal further.

Riding Off Into the Sunset

Soon after the original meeting with the vice president and director, I was aggressively wooed by another brokerage firm who took my proposal seriously. Their attitude was, "Hey, if you know how to make more money, tell us what you need and we'll provide the environment in which you can operate at peak capacity." It was a very pure, capitalistic attitude and exactly the type of atmosphere we were looking for.

I decided to jump ship and swim towards a safer harbor—another major Wall Street firm—for the next phase of my business career.

New Business Unfolds

For the next month or so I was busy weeding through my 2,000-plus accounts. I knew I had to streamline my business in order to specialize in managing money and to spend more time educating clients. After I was settled in and began my investment management business, I told my new employer that my larger accounts needed individualized professional money managers, not simply a mutual fund. And even though the firm had a capital management department which handled accounts of $1 million and up for the affluent and for institutions, there were no provisions for the middle market—the $100,000 to $1,000,000 account. I felt strongly that individual investors should receive the same special treatment as the Fortune 500 companies received. Even though my investment philosophy wasn't new to the firm, they couldn't justify setting up a new division or department just for me.

I felt as though I had just slammed into another brick wall in my just-blossoming career in growth account management. But I was undaunted and determined as ever, and it was during dinner on one of the sales contest junkets that John and I earned, that the answer finally came to me. It lit up our table like a 1,000-watt floodlight—a few important words that I had known all along: Lump Sum Distributions. And these words would eventually help make my dream become a reality.

Earlier, during a pre-retirement seminar, I happened to meet a woman representing a large savings and loan institution who gave in-house corporate presentations to employees on the subject of lump sum distributions— retirement fund proceeds distributed to retiring employees. And since I had authored a major publication on IRA rollovers, I took the opportunity to introduce myself to this woman as a fellow safe-investment enthusiast. At one point during our conversation about investments, I offered a business proposition. I said, "Elizabeth, if you want to sell your stocks through me, I absolutely promise you I won't solicit your customers. I will facilitate you by setting up an account. The customer brings the stock to you, you sell through me and I make sure the customer gets professional attention." Elizabeth knew that otherwise she'd tell her customers to see their own broker to sell the stocks and send the check back to her. Well, she also knew how many times brokers would try to keep that customer from taking that lump sum, which would be $400 to $500,000, back to her. So I told

"My logical mind said that if I sold investments that worked, I wouldn't lose 70 percent of my clients."

Elizabeth that instead of subjecting her potential customers to being cut off at the pass, I would help her. She agreed, and Elizabeth and her firm became my largest customers.

I suggested to John that we invite Elizabeth to become a third partner. John asked why I thought she would want to. I said, "Well, John, she is an employee and is probably earning in the neighborhood of $35,000 to $40,000 a year. If we could explain to her how much more she could make by bringing all her depositors—with an average of $2 to $3 million in deposits a month—to us, she would earn 10 times her salary. Also, that would give us the ammunition we needed to get the approval to set up an investment management department."

Needless to say, after a pleasant evening of dinner and comparing notes with Elizabeth, she agreed to join us. Thirty days later we combined our accounts totaling $5 million with her $5 million customer deposits and that $10 million was the opening balance for the newly-created department that became our firm's Special Accounts department. Now we were armed and ready to take on the world of professional money management. What I learned over the next 10 years was enough to fill a book!

Now beginning with the next chapter we'll go back in time a little bit and I'll tell you about the three words that changed the way I looked at the world of investing.

3

The Human Nature Flaw: Why You Can't Get Ahead in the Stock Market

"Making money is as easy as losing weight, i.e., buying low and selling high is just as easy as exercising more and eating less."

—*Charles Fahy*

It was the end of 1977. The bull market was raging. Profit-takers were in and out of the market, running with their money. Many long-term investors were also cashing in on the opportunities. Everyone seemed to be making money on the upswing. Why, then, were my clients losing money at every turn?

Earlier in my career, I rationalized that the poor performance was unquestionably due to a flat or down market—-I blamed the market for everything at that time. I started analyzing every step I took. My research was impeccable; my firm's research was untouchable and I was happy with my stock picks. I was doing everything right—servicing my clients, giving the best investment advice I could. What could possibly be going wrong? What was it that wasn't working in the investment process?

Finally, after what seemed a lifetime of agonizing, the only logical answer kept surfacing. And it was so obvious. Three words that had evaded me for years: "Human Nature Flaw." A critical link in the chain of successful investing, this obstacle had to be dealt with.

> ❞ discovered that human nature was and always will be in direct conflict with successful investing."

The statistics proved it time and again, and often by their own admissions. The investors themselves proved it: human beings have basic flaws. Now, let me explain how I mean that.

The stock market seemed to breed impatience, fear, greed, and, during good cycles, these factors ran rampant. I saw fortunes won and lost in the wink of an eye. Human nature was a treacherous force to be reckoned with. The major problem was that investors were buying stocks high and selling them low.

I discovered that human nature was and always will be in direct conflict with successful investing. I realized then and there I had to do something to harness the emotional roller coaster ride my clients were on. Otherwise, human nature would dominate the investment decision process and make it impossible to show any consistent positive returns in the portfolio.

Ozzie and Harriet Invest

Let me illustrate the cause and effect of human nature with a typical story I like to tell prospective investors during my seminars. I call it, "Ozzie and Harriet Invest."

Ozzie came home feeling like a 'big shot,' walked straight to the kitchen and told his wife, Harriet, he had just bought a great stock at $10 a share. Harriet asked why it was so great. He explained that his golfing buddy's stockbroker said it was at $2 six months ago. They said the company invented a new product and it sailed to $10 a share and would go to $15 a share in a year. They claimed they'd make 50 percent on their money, buying now.

Harriet's next question was "Where did you get the money to buy the stock?" He sheepishly explained he got it from Ricky and David's college fund. Harriet fumed at the idea that he would take conservative, hard-earned money and put it in something as speculative as the stock market.

Now, what's the first thing that happens when you buy stock? It goes down! Sure enough, Ozzie's great $10 stock went down to $8. Ozzie came home and found Harriet in a horrible mood. She was slamming the oven door, silverware, pots, and pans. She threw Ozzie's dinner on the table, just missing his lap.

"What's wrong, dear?" he asked.

"What's wrong?" she retorted. "I saw the stock listings today and that 'great stock' of yours is down to $8 and you just lost 20 percent of the college savings for our boys," she blasted. "You sell that stock now, before you lose it all, or your next dinner won't miss your lap!"

So, sure enough, the next day Ozzie sold the stock. The stockbroker made commissions on the buy and sale, and Ozzie lost two points and both commissions. Now, what happens when we sell a stock? It goes up! Sure enough, the stock went back up and hit $12 a share.

So Ozzie came home, slammed the front door, threw his briefcase down and stormed into the kitchen. Harriet was alarmed by his hostility.

"What's wrong, dear?" she asked.

"That stock you made me sell is now up to $12," he grumped. He now emphasized that he knew what he was doing, and that when it came to investing, he wore the pants in the family. Harriet accommodated him and agreed. The next day he bought it back in at $12 a share.

Know what happened next? Right. The stock went down over the next few months to $10 a share. Now, he came home rather solemn, but, Harriet was sympathetic and they talked about how frustrating stocks were. So far, the broker had made three commissions, they had a loss and both were saying they would have been better off in Certificates of Deposit (CDs) at the bank.

They decided to sell the stock. They sold at $10 a share with the broker making yet a fourth commission. Now what happened after they sold the stock? Right. It went up. Their $10 stock moved to $15 a share.

In the last scene, Ozzie and Harriet were reassuring themselves that they were right; the brokers made money, people didn't, and the whole market was rigged by those Wall Street types.

However, if they had stayed with the game plan or set up some basic rules—like a business plan with cycles—they could have made a profit. If Ozzie had a systematic stock investing account, he could have bought continuously and would have done even better. Even the "toss of the coin" system, which I'll explain later in the chapter, would have been a good system.

I'd Rather Fight Than Switch

Human nature is a bigger problem than managing the stocks. It is so much easier to follow your fears and joys than your common business sense, especially when the market is going crazy. But it is a discipline that must be followed in order to work within the system.

A visual example of this roller coaster is pictured on the following page (Figure 3-1). This is a lighthearted, yet realistic look at greed and fear in the marketplace.

I always return to the theory, though, that if we resist these human urges and simply hold for longer terms—or take the time to understand these tendencies—we will shine as winners more often than not.

For example, let's take a look at our corporate retirement accounts. They are solid, steady, growing assets. Yet, our individual portfolios fail to succeed like the pension or benefit accounts do. As a matter of fact, individuals often fail to surpass a CD rate of return. How can this be?

Simple.

Figure 3-1 Human Nature and Stocks Greed/Fear Chart

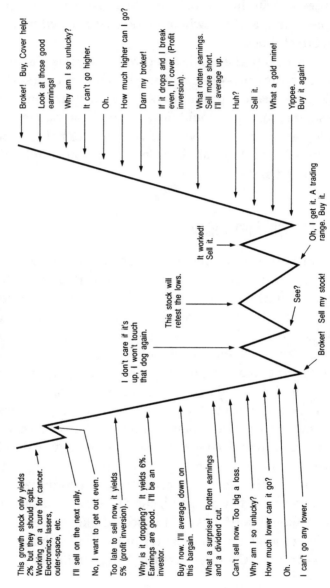

It is not as easy to switch, or jump in and out, with a pension or corporate benefit plan as it is with an individual portfolio. The human nature factor is bypassed and the money isn't touched until retirement. What is at work with these less personally managed accounts is the bypassing of human nature flaws and the use of a systematic, consistent approach to investing. Using these, time is on the investor's side.

I have an investor I call my "wealthiest client," and he is a living example of the invest-and-forget philosophy. Joe is a 40-year veteran foreman for a crew of dock workers for a major oil corporation and had strained his back while at work. In pain, he went to a lawyer demanding a lawsuit against the company for medical attention. The lawyer was surprised that Joe was not aware of his company's medical benefits and asked why he was not using his medical coverage for his immediate needs. Joe didn't know anything about his benefits. The lawyer asked Joe to bring his quarterly benefit computer run to his office so they could study it together. As the lawyer reviewed the benefits package, he was shocked to find that Joe's benefits added up to approximately $565,000. He asked Joe how much he earned to which Joe replied $27,500 a year. His lawyer said, "Joe, you're 65 years old and you are entitled to Social Security benefits now and also you have over half a million dollars. You could be getting three times what you earn now if you retired tomorrow!"

Needless to say, Joe was shocked by the revelation and explained humbly that he could not read and only had a fifth grade education. He went on to explain that he didn't know what Social Security was and he certainly didn't understand that he had a half million dollars. The lawyer then sent Joe to see me.

After Joe and I had the good fortune to meet, we went over his financial affairs and I had the pleasure of telling him that he could retire now and receive about $75,000 a year! I was curious to know what his perception of this sudden financial success was, so I asked him how he thought he had accomplished this. Here was his humble response:

> **H** aving a system is a critical ingredient in the success of your portfolio."

"I know I'm ignorant," he began, "but I remember about 30 years ago, the company sent me some forms and there were three boxes on each form. One box had a number (5), one box had a number (10) and one box had a number (15). Now, I'm not that dumb. I know 15 percent on your money is better than five percent. So, I put my X on the number (15) box."

What Joe didn't understand was that the box wasn't an interest question; it was a question of what percentage of salary to withhold from the paycheck to buy company stock! This fine gentleman had been socking away 15 percent of his salary in a tax-deferred stock purchase plan for the last 30 years. He wasn't earning $27,500; he was earning about $32,000. His capital appreciated and the sheer compounding value of accumulation built the benefits to a half million dollars. An approximate re-creation can be seen in Figure 3-2 and Table 3-1.

The moral to the story is that a long-term, systematic, tax-deferred, compounding, dollar-cost-averaging, accumulating stock account can make up for a lot of ignorance. And human nature is not a threat if the money is not touched.

To further illustrate the stock accummulation system, the human nature factor is evident in the well-known "dart" portfolio method or "Random Walk" portfolio theory. In both of these cases, a random or blind approach is used to pick stocks, yet the discipline of using a "system" plus long-term holding eliminates the human factor of trying to out-think, out-analyze, and out-maneuver the market.

Having a system is a critical ingredient in the success of your portfolio. Sometimes, it makes no difference which system you use, as long as you use it consistently.

Figure 3-2   The Advantages of Periodic Savings

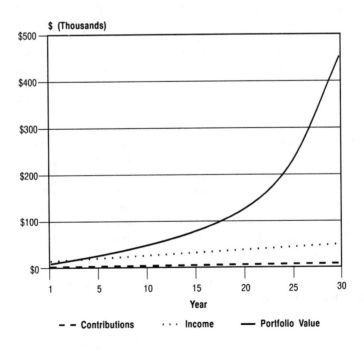

Table 3-1   The Advantages of Periodic Savings

Year	Salary	Contribution	Investment Return	Portfolio Value
1	$10,000	$1,500	$0	$1,500
2	$10,500	$1,575	$165	$3,075
3	$11,025	$1,654	$338	$5,067
4	$11,576	$1,736	$557	$7,361
5	$12,155	$1,823	$810	$9,994
6	$12,763	$1,914	$1,099	$13,007
7	$13,401	$2,010	$1,431	$16,448
8	$14,071	$2,111	$1,809	$20,368
9	$14,775	$2,216	$2,241	$24,825
10	$15,513	$2,327	$2,731	$29,883
11	$16,289	$2,443	$3,287	$35,613
12	$17,103	$2,566	$3,917	$42,096
13	$17,959	$2,694	$4,631	$49,421
14	$18,856	$2,828	$5,436	$57,685
15	$19,799	$2,970	$6,345	$67,001
16	$20,789	$3,118	$7,370	$77,489
17	$21,829	$3,274	$8,524	$89,287
18	$22,920	$3,438	$9,822	$102,547
19	$24,066	$3,610	$11,280	$117,437
20	$25,270	$3,790	$12,918	$134,146
21	$26,533	$3,980	$14,756	$152,882
22	$27,860	$4,179	$16,817	$173,878
23	$29,253	$4,388	$19,127	$197,392
24	$30,715	$4,607	$21,713	$223,712
25	$32,251	$4,838	$24,608	$253,158
26	$33,864	$5,080	$27,847	$286,085
27	$35,557	$5,334	$31,469	$322,888
28	$37,335	$5,600	$35,518	$364,006
29	$39,201	$5,880	$40,041	$409,927
30	$41,161	$6,174	$45,092	$461,193

Assumes 15% contributions of salary, 11% investment income, and 5% annual pay increases.

Chuck the Research and Flip a Coin?

I make a shocking example of a systems presentation at one of my seminars that leaves audiences laughing at themselves. At the beginning of the lecture, I will stack armloads of business and financial publications on the table next to me. I'll include *Time, Fortune, Forbes, Money*, the *Wall Street Journal, Barron's*—all the heavy-hitting magazines and papers I can find. I look right at my audience and say, "All of these publications contain information you need to know to research investment ideas. And you pour over them every week. Lots of reading, isn't it?" Then I pull out a couple of technical stock charting newsletters and investment books and throw those on top of the pile and say, "And, you will need statistics, historical performance, and technical data to add perspective." Then, I might add a few books on fundamentals and continue stacking material a mile high.

Then, I put a portable TV on top and look square into the audience and say, "Don't forget the financial news network and the local investment talk shows—you can't miss these."

Well, by now my audience is probably thinking I've gone mad as I point out that with all of this reading, calculating, and researching, less than 20 percent will ever make any money with these methods. You may as well flip a coin, because with a coin you will win 50 percent of the time. You see, the simple truth is, the coin is objective and utilizes a system—in the most raw sense—and will be right half the time. It does not fall prey to human nature. All the reading and researching in the world is great, if it utilizes a system. But, unfortunately, what happens in most cases is that people will chuck all of their research on a hot stock tip or short-term profit-taking in a bull market. Of course, I'm not advocating that you toss a coin in deciding which way to go with your investment portfolio, but a basic truth is illustrated in favor of the use of a system.

Work the System!

In the early 70s, I read an issue of one of the major business magazines in which Alan Greenspan wrote a one-page essay on how to run the U.S. government's financial system. On the opposite page was an essay written by Milton Friedman on the same topic. Was I dismayed! I thought, after I read both stories, here were two Ph.Ds, one a Nobel prize winner for Economics, two presidential advisors who could not agree with each other on how to run our government's financial program. How in the world could an individual investor possibly have a chance of finding the winning combination to investing if these two brilliant men couldn't even agree on one?

My question was answered a few years later when I had the opportunity to meet with Dr. Friedman. He gave me a simple, yet brilliant, explanation. He said that Greenspan's system was fine and that it worked. He said his own system was different, but was just as fine and that it also worked. Both systems would work equally well. The problem, he explained, was that Congress, in trying to find an economic vehicle or system from which to go from point A to point B, made their vehicle from parts of various systems. Their "system" was like a vehicle made with parts of a bicycle, VW engine, tank treads, boat, and airplane parts. Then they wondered why it wouldn't work!

His advice was get a cohesive plan, implement it and stay with it. Then it will work just fine.

What you see with both the Greenspan/Friedman and the Ozzie and Harriet stories is that a system works if you work your system.

David Dreman, managing director of Dreman Value Management, Inc., Investment Counsel in New York and author of *The New Contrarian Investment Strategy,* wrote in the February 20, 1989 issues of *Forbes* magazine, "One of the peculiarities of the market—or human nature, really—is that most investors don't learn from past mistakes. I'm referring to everyday errors repeated constantly. It seems that you can correct a golf slice or improve a bad tennis serve, but in markets, no matter how much time or experience most investors have, they repeat their flubs time and again."

He went on to say, "Investors repeatedly jump ship on a good strategy just because it hasn't worked so well lately and, almost invariably, abandon it at precisely the wrong time.

"If a method has worked well over the years and you are comfortable with it, stick to it through the period it's not doing so great, even if it's for as long as a year or two. Sure, it's ridiculous to think that any strategy is going to work every quarter or every year. Superior investment results aren't achieved on a quarterly or even an annual basis," he says.

Mr. Dreman went on to explain that John Templeton, one of the greatest value investment managers of all time, whose record is almost unmatched over the decades, has had occasions when even his stocks have under-performed the averages for long periods of time—and in some cases for up to four years before surging ahead. But investors who deserted him in his poor period have mostly lived to regret their decisions.

Is It Sport or Is It Safety?

Human nature also rears its head whenever a discussion turns to speculating versus investing. Speculators are victims of the elements of human nature because they thrive on the thrill of the roll of the dice—the uncertainty, the dangers, the all-or-nothing mentality. Speculators—or traders—in my opinion are looking to make a quick buck. And, that's fine, if you can afford to take risks. But to me, these people are ego machines and are always living life on the edge of risk.

Speculators love the sport of playing the stock market. It's a form of entertainment for them. They juggle their capital in and out of the market, generating nice commissions for the broker. The speculator has absolutely no plan, no long-range strategy for investing.

The conservative investor, however, wants and needs a plan. This investor needs to satisfy his comfort factor. He has executed a long-term system, much like a business plan that is adhered to through all market cycles—and he watches his capital grow steadily. Again, the speculator is emotionally-driven, wagged around by human nature. The conservative investor, on the other hand, is driven by the logic of the system.

The problem with Wall Street, as I see it, is that it loves a speculator. Speculators keep the capital liquid and flowing. There's no doubt in my mind that if I had 500 speculator clients, I would make quite a bit more money. But, I happen to know that if I give these 500 speculators enough time, they'll financially hang themselves. Then, after all is said and done, they'll probably blame me for not taking the rope away from them!

The only professional speculator I have ever heard of who made it big was Richard Dennis, the king of commod-

**Stockbrokers and clients respond to
human nature, *not* wisdom!**

©Cartoonists' and Writers Syndicate

ities speculation. He took an original investment of $5,000 and parlayed it into a net worth of $100 million. He continued to play the market and eventually lost half of his $100 million. So, he got smart and retired at age 45. Curious thing though, he had a degree in Psychology!

Most of the time speculators are so hard-headed they won't listen to reason, no matter what. But that's where many ethical brokers get stuck. They want to service their clients, make them happy, execute the trades they request— but the brokers get burned in the process, because they eventually lose the customer.

I learned a long time ago that I can't control people and I certainly can't control Wall Street—nor do I want to. Those who try are on the road to self-destruction. Rather, I like to think of myself as a buffer to help investors handle the emotional roller coasters they ride from time to time. That's why my business works as well as it does. I've taken the human nature factor out of portfolio management. That's why I'm proud to say that I didn't lose any customers during the 1987 crash or the 1990 Persian Gulf Crisis.

Now, I can't point the finger at human nature and blast every individual investor out there for not having a system, not having patience to hold on long-term, for giving in to fear and greed—no. Wall Street plays a major part in the care and feeding of human nature. The recipes it cooks up are tempting and hard to resist, but the heartburn is a killer.

Let's talk more about investment programs that sizzle like bacon, but clog your portfolio's lifeline, in the next few chapters.

4

The Bond Sizzle: Wall Street Meets Madison Avenue

"I can guarantee you 50% return of your money in 24 hours: If you give me a dollar today and come by tomorrow I'll give you .50 of your dollar!
—Charles Fahy

You see them advertised on television. You read about them in full-color ads in respectable magazines and newspapers. Your next-door neighbor owns some, as do your doctors and your second cousin. Seems like wherever you turn, someone is talking about them. What are they?

Bonds.

You might say that everyone is jumping on the "Bond Wagon." They're promoted as "safe, tax-free, high-yielding, and commission-free." What else could you possibly ask for in an investment?

Well, for a change, how about the truth about this outrageous investment product? For example, how about the fact that bonds historically have been poor performers and that inflation erodes the invested capital over time? And what about the confusing information on taxable equivalent charts used by marketers of tax-free bonds to entice investors? Plus, how about the truth that bonds should not be bought and held by individuals, like stocks, but traded by skilled professionals? (See Figure 4-1)

The professional managers are constantly evaluating the interest rates of the world economies. They also must evaluate factors such as international monetary policy over and above the U.S. domestic policies. Each country's monetary strategy plays a vital role and impacts on our own bond markets. The issuer of bonds, such as the U.S. government or a corporation, is a credit factor in itself. Therefore, the skilled professional has to understand the financial details of the issuing company not unlike that of the professional stock picker. The major difference, which tends to compound the problem with bonds, is that historically, unlike stocks, bonds lose value due to inflation. Time works against the bond investor. Now, add that to the complexity of the ever-changing fluctuations of interest rates!

A simple rule for understanding bonds is that when interest rates rise, bond prices fall and vice-versa. This is

Figure 4-1   'Boring' Bonds? They've Been More Volatile Than Stocks

During the 1980s, the corporate bond market was more volatile than the sotck market. The fluctuation in bonds increased sharply after October 1979, when the Federal Reserve adopted a policy allowing wider moves in short-term interest rates. Since then, returns in the bond market generally have varied more than in the stock market, according to the volatility indexes compiled by Shearson Lehman Economics. The highest peak shows a period when bonds were seven times as volatile as stocks. Bonds settled down considerably in late 1986, and stocks have fluctuated more since October of 1987. But, as fears about the dollar's decline and accelerating inflation permeate the fixed-income markets, the volatility of bonds is picking up again.

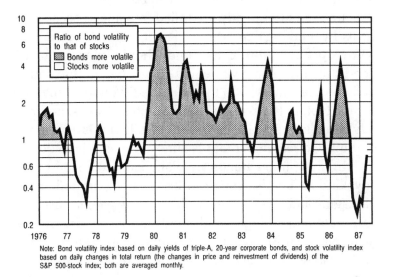

Note: Bond volatility index based on daily yields of triple-A, 20-year corporate bonds, and stock volatility index based on daily changes in total return (the changes in price and reinvestment of dividends) of the S&P 500-stock index; both are averaged monthly.

Note: Bond volatility index based on daily yields of triple-A, 20-year corporate bonds, and stock volatility index based on daily changes in total return (the change in price and reinvestment of dividends) of the S&P 500-stock index; both are averaged monthly.

SOURCE: Shearson Lehman Brothers Inc.

true of all bonds regardless of how they are rated or whether or not they are backed by the U.S. government.

The Bond Lullaby

The marketing trick being played on the public is that while the government bonds are backed by the full faith and credit of the government, a mutual fund actively manages bonds and their performance is a result of how smart the money manager is. The performance of the manager is not guaranteed by the U.S. government, as can be implied.

Investors frequently are lulled into a false sense of security by thinking that a diversified bond fund, for example, will reduce risk. But, if the fund's holdings are primarily bonds, then the share value will still be tied to fluctuations in the interest rates. Don't get caught. If you must invest in bonds, look at the economy and at interest rates, and only buy when interest rates are likely to fall. This is a good rule of thumb to remember, but is almost impossible to do.

In my opinion, bonds are plain bad news. And I mean any kind of bonds. They can be wrapped around snazzy packaging and fancy names such as municipals, tax-exempts, corporate bonds, high-yield bond mutual funds, Government National Mortgage Association units, zero coupons, unit trusts, and on and on. But bonds are bonds are bonds. They are all the same and they can be misunderstood. Marketing techniques used when advertising these bond products are designed to perpetuate this misunderstanding. Ads encourage the consumer to focus attention on specific numbers that sound appealing, therefore leading the investor to assume that those particular numbers pertain to bottom line return. The fact is, they rarely do. I am not alone in my harsh view of bonds. In Carter Randall's book, *Up on the Market*, (Chicago: Probus, 1992) he says, "Bonds represent, in effect, legalized confiscation of capital . . . the securities industry has issued a plethora of shares of bond funds in recent years. These are mutual funds or investment trusts that invest in bonds, running the gamut from US Treasury bonds and corporate bonds, to tax-exempt bonds and junk bonds. My recommendation is that they, too, should be avoided."

Focus on the Fine Print

The main thing most investors want to know about is what the bottom line return or "total return" on an investment will be. However, total return is rarely used to market bonds. The numbers shown in the brochures are usually the "dividend interest yield," not the bottom line total return, unless—conveniently—interest rates have been going down. The dividend yield is important, but it can be dramatically adjusted when additional data are taken into consideration. Only by reading and computing the data in small print can the total return be determined.

Total return is the sum of the dividend yield and the capital gain or capital loss of the investment. Say that a bond shows a dividend rate of 10%. If an investment has experienced a capital decline of –15%, the total return is –5%, not the +10% as insinuated by the brochure.

Here's another example. Sure-Fire Investments advertises a dividend rate of 10.14%. The fine print, however, states that the value of the shares was $10 last year and is $9 currently, a 10% capital loss of value in the shares. The conclusion is as illustrated:

10.14%	Dividend Yield
-10.00%	Capital Loss
.14%	Total Return

This example shows how a 10.14% dividend yield turns into a .14% total return at bottom line, before factoring in commission costs.

Other bogus marketing techniques are used to inflate presumed market investment returns. For those readers who are in the securities business, the following information will probably ring very true. For the less sophisticated investor, though, it's important that you pay particular attention to these next few paragraphs.

A yield for a certain short period of time—say seven days—is not a true indication of the yield that will be produced over one year or five years. An embellished yield figure can be created by dividing the dividend by a lower current share value, and also by neglecting to compute the commission cost to purchase the shares. For example, if over the last twelve months you purchased an investment that paid 10 percent in dividends, declined in market value 4 percent and cost 6 percent to purchase, the twelve-month return on your investment would be zero percent.

To put it a little more clearly, the enhanced yield figures you read about are a result of strategies used to specifically increase the yield for a stated period of time. An example could be various option-writing techniques. The net profitable premium would enhance the yield of the portfolio. Hedging techniques are also used to boost the yield. These two examples are not usually discussed in the marketing brochure, but are extremely important factors for you to understand when looking at yield, simply because these two techniques can also work *against t*he portfolio, negatively affecting the performance. These are some of the risk factors outlined in the prospectus.

Unfair Comparisons

Many times, the bond packagers will disclose excellent performance figures using a five-year historical rate of return. Many took advantage of the five-year period of July 1987–July 1992, which showed a superior return as compared to the stock market for that same period of time. Confidence was at an all-time high for the bond promoters. Why? The answer is simple. The bond market did extraordinarily well those past five years. Look at the stock market over those past five years: the Dow was at its peak in 1987, then the market crashed in October of 1987. We had a flat market in 1988; 1990 brought the Gulf war, 1991 was a good year, but 1992 was a slow year. These five years in the stock market had the second worst year this century—1987. How can the worst compare with the best? Comparing that five-year bond period with our stock market climate is outrageously unfair and unjustifiable, in my opinion. Duping the individual investor with these clouded statistics so freely is imprudent. This bond scenario is not likely to duplicate itself in our lifetime and thinking it will is preposterous!

Buy American?

Also giving investments entrancing names that summon up impressions of safety, stability, and infallibility is another dubious marketing technique. Remember the bacon analogy? It looks, sounds and smells good cooking in the pan, and it tastes good, but eat enough of it and it will kill you! Classic in that category is the Government National Mortgage Association (GNMA). Sounds great, doesn't it? A GNMA or Ginnie Mae is a debt security issued by a specific government agency. Ginnie Mae securities are sold in order to acquire funds for FHA/VA guaranteed mortgages. An investor who buys a GNMA is acquiring a part of the pool of mortgage loans. The title is intended to suggest complete safety, yet, according to industry sources, it ranked number three in 1986 for scandalous investments. The federal government does insure the repayment of the principal, but there is no guarantee of the market risk of the principal. Also, not pointed out is the purchasing power risk due to inflation! GNMAs are also fixed-income securities and will decline in value as interest rates go up, resulting in a capital loss.

Included in the rate of return promoted is not just the interest, but the principal and interest. GNMAs are mortgage instruments just like the mortgage on your home where you pay a monthly dollar amount that represents your interest and a portion of your principal. Therefore, you need to ascertain whether the yield being promoted in the sale of GNMAs is, in fact, either the *interest* on your money or the *rate of return* on your money. If it is the rate of return, then you are receiving interest plus some of your money back. If you don't know the difference and you spend what you collect, you could own the investment until it is worth zero. When investors realize they have been collecting and spending their own money thinking it was interest, they have a nasty habit of suing the broker who sold the product to them. The brokerage industry is loaded with these kinds of lawsuits.

Investors who have locked up high-yielding GNMAs or other bonds face a logical problem when interest rates decline—they can't enjoy the benefits of the high rate due to the risk of having to re-finance. This is why one must be sophisticated enough to understand bonds and to also know how to trade them when the time comes.

In addition, commonly used terms are "trust," "high-yield," or even "Federal Government Investment No. 1412"—meaning "look investor at how many we've done before! Over 1,400!" The reference to huge quantities is another tool of embellishing. The firm that sells the most of a product does not necessarily mean that the product earns profit for the buyer. It's human nature to make the presumption that because so much of it is sold, it must be good. That's the old American "big=good" delusion many of us suffer from.

Some marketing is quite ingenious. For example, by implying that an investment firm is successful, we automatically infer that its customers will also be successful. Just remember that even though in 1929 many investment firms made a profit, that wasn't necessarily the case for their customers! I remember some years back one of Hollywood's most well-known TV and movie stars (and a wealthy business tycoon) did a series of TV commercials for a major Wall Street brokerage firm in which he touted that the "firm" had been profitable since 1929. A very subtle way of saying that you will also make money if you invest your money with this firm. Madison Avenue's subliminal seduction at its best. Guess who's really making the money?

Bonds, Bundling, and Baloney

Meanwhile, sales of tax-exempt unit trusts in the first two months of 1991 were reported up 58 percent to $1.06 billion. But while unit investment trusts offer diversity and professional selection, they carry high fees. They also may contain bonds that can be "called" (redeemed) before scheduled maturity. This could reduce yield. While there is a secondary or resale market, investors who use it may get less or more than they paid for their trust units. Because of market fluctuations, a yield is far from a sure thing. Even if investors hold to maturity, they may be getting a lot less interest than they could elsewhere. Defaults and bond calls can significantly reduce the anticipated return of a unit investment trust. Likewise, zero coupon bonds called before maturity (and while still at a deep discount) can significantly reduce expected yield.

Bond packagers routinely come to market with new unit trusts. The secondary market isn't for the uninitiated, however. The individual investor buying in the secondary market may think he is getting a bargain when, in fact, these products are leftovers from poorly-performing portfolios. It's known in the industry as "bundling." Bundling boosts yield and disguises the weaker bonds. If these bonds were sold individually, most investors would shy away from them as unsuitable investments.

My main beef about tax-exempt bonds is that there exists an almost-utopian environment in which to sell them. That's not to say there are no controls, but everyone knows that the "sizzle" sells. Then the power of greed steps in— even more so with the power of the "tax-free" angle. It's wanting to get something for nothing, or to beat the government. To be able to go to a cocktail party and tell your friends you are in tax-exempts can be a real ego trip. It's the same as saying, "Let me take a look at my gold Rolex watch and give you the time; or let me drop by your house in my Rolls." It's a form of product "name-dropping" and a status symbol as well. I haven't met a doctor yet who hasn't told me he's in tax-exempts. It's a socially acceptable way to brag about

having wealth. But it's a lot of bull, and Wall Street understands that. If investors would take the same money they
put into tax-exempts and put it into growth stocks, then
leave the doggone things alone, the money would work a
heck of a lot better for them than in the municipals even
after taxes!

Now let's talk about the confusion surrounding the tax
equivalent charts which the tax-exempt bond fund people
use to sell to the unsuspecting public.

First, the whole bond scene has been clouded with this
confusion about tax equivalent tables. I maintain that these
charts are little more than a sales gimmick and the most
important tool to hook investors into buying tax-exempts.
Consider a scenario in which you are told that if you get a
7 percent tax-free bond it is the tax equivalent of 10 percent,
if you are in a 30 percent tax bracket. This is pure nonsense;
obviously we all have deductions. Gross income is irrele-
vant; what counts is the size of your adjusted net income.
Take your net taxes and divide by your gross income and
you get your effective tax bracket. For example, if your
income was $100,000 and your taxes were $20,000, you ef-
fectively pay a 20 percent tax. I have found, as a matter of
fact, that indeed around 20 percent is what most of us pay.
It changes the bond seller's arithmetic substantially and re-
veals that these tax equivalent charts can be totally misleading for the average investor.

Wall Street Meets Madison Avenue

So, if everything said above is true, why does the investing
public continue to be duped? Let's take a look at where I
think the trouble starts. I call it "Wall Street Meets Madison
Avenue."

The country's largest promoters of bond funds is a crafty combination of the talents of savvy Wall Street product technicians and the snap, crackle, pop of advertising wordsmiths. Marketers with big sales promotion budgets produce tens of thousands of dollars worth of sales "slicks"—brochures featuring full-color photos of American flags and eagles and reeking of patriotic symbolism. Along with the expensive, impressive promo piece is a smaller, fairly dull-looking booklet filled with microscopic print only someone with a law degree would even attempt to read. We all should, though. This is the prospectus, or the heart of the product where everything should be spelled out in black and white. Throw away the glossy distraction piece. The dull-looking booklet is uninviting for a reason: they don't expect you to read it.

To illustrate, let's take a look at a bond fund prospectus published by a leading supplier of tax-exempt bond funds. First, check the table of contents. Your first clue that something is not quite right is that "risk" is not listed on the table. This means the writer of the prospectus is forcing you to read every word until you finally find anything remotely connected to risk. Finally, in the last third of the prospectus you come to a section titled: "Net Asset Value." Look carefully at this section. In the last paragraph, last sentence, you read the following: "Net asset value generally increases when interest rates decline and decreases when interest rates rise." If you don't know what you are looking for, you will probably read right past this. Most people who are not in the business don't understand the sentence anyway. So if you invest in this product and start to lose money, you feel you haven't been treated fairly or weren't told the facts. Then you might want to talk to a lawyer about recouping your losses on the grounds that information was withheld and you couldn't make an informed decision. The lawyer will probably ask if you read the prospectus and you will then say that you tried to. What the lawyer will most likely say at that point is that you received the prospectus, read it, should have known what you were getting into, and therefore you lose. Yes folks, this is entirely legal.

We've Been Duped!

Many investors naively rely completely on their financial advisor to give them full disclosure on all products. Trouble is—and they don't like to admit it—these advisors sometimes just don't know what they ought to. The same kind of trickery described above in the "slicks" and the prospectuses is played on those of us in the industry, too. For example, I recently attended a sales luncheon hosted by a large marketer of tax-exempt bond funds. The only reason I went was to find out what tricks the marketer was up to now. Sure enough, the bond fund marketer was represented by a very attractive young female wholesaler who just parroted everything she learned in training about the bond fund. All the guys at the lunch were goo-goo eyed over her and probably didn't hear a word she said. She talked about everything being documented in the prospectus, but never mentioned a word about risk. That was typical. It was the blind leading the blind.

In 1976, I took part in a training program for new brokers. At that time, I was the regional director for annuity sales. I arrived early for the program, just in time to hear the New York bond expert speak at the conference. As I listened I thought, "Hey, here's a fresh, green batch of recruits to screw up with all of this bond talk." I was sitting in the back of the audience and I raised my hand. The speaker recognized me and said, "Yes, Charlie, you have a question?" I said, "Yes, will you explain to these guys what happens when interest rates go up?" And he squirmed a little and answered, "Well, Charlie, that's quite a complex question. Since you and I are having lunch in a few minutes, why don't I explain it to you then?" So I said, "No, I already understand what happens. I think the trainees ought to know, though." I could tell I was making him very uncomfortable and needless to say, the question was never answered in the session. Fortunately for that group, when it was my turn to speak after lunch I educated them very quickly that deferred annuities enjoy increases in yield as interest rates rise, but bonds lose value as interest rates rise.

The Bond Graveyard

Many stockbrokers have to hard-sell or convince the investor at the point of sale when promoting bonds. Then they have to go back and explain several years down the road why it's not working. Then they lose the customer, more than likely because money was lost. But salespeople of tax-exempt securities just go and find new bodies. Can you imagine going to work and facing your clients after you sold them this junk, when interest rates are sky high and their fund is trading at 50 cents on the dollar? What in the heck are you supposed to say about this "safe" investment?

It goes on all the time. The average broker made about $98,000 in 1991, so why not? It's lucrative and easy to sell bonds, and brokers make decent commissions on them. The sad thing is that many brokers don't realize that bonds are bad when they sell them and only find out after it's too late and they lose a client.

Here's an example of how a typical sale of tax-exempts is made to an unsophisticated individual investor.

Mr. Jones visits his broker and complains about his high taxes. The broker asks Mr. Jones if he's heard about tax-exempts. Mr. Jones says, "Gee, I thought tax-exempt bonds were just for rich people like doctors and lawyers." The broker answers, "Oh no, you can buy them in unit trusts for as little as $1,000 an instrument. That will put you in a pooled account with the big money. You see, the tax-exempt market is open to the smaller investor and you have $50,000, so that's perfect." Then Mr. Jones says, "Is it safe?" The broker answers, "Of course, Mr. Jones. You're talking about state municipals guaranteed by the issuing agency."

The broker then says, "Now you have an instrument that is paying eight percent tax-free. The tax equivalent from that means you'd have to earn about eleven percent from a CD." Then the broker will pull out a 12-month performance chart, but what good does that do? You absolutely must look at 10-, 20-, and 30-year performance charts to see the truth. Then you will see the tremendous erosion of capital from inflation. The rate you buy at today is what you are stuck with for the next 20 years. When the customer asks about risk, and just the past 12 months is discussed, the customer is not getting full disclosure.

But I Don't Want a Raise!

Let me put it another way. I wonder how many readers of this book went to work 20 years ago and demanded from their employers to have a fixed income for the life of their careers? It sounds like a dumb question, but if you buy a General Motors bond, for example, and it pays 9 percent for 20 years, you've just told GM that you want a 9 percent fixed on your capital for the next 20 years, a totally illogical investment!

Peter Lynch comments on bonds as a safe investment: "... They aren't. People who sleep better at night because they own bonds and not stocks are suseptable to rude awakenings—unlike wine and baseball cards, money is cheapened with age."[1]

In the beginning of my career I used to sell taxable and tax-free unit investment trusts before I realized the shocking truth about them. I bought them for myself, my family, my friends, and my clients. Then, in church a couple of years later, some of my friends would scoot over next to me in the church pew to ask me what was going wrong with the funds. It got to the point that it was a bummer to go to church!

At least I did buy the bonds for myself, which showed that I really believed in what I was selling and wasn't just after commission bucks.

Dismal Performers and Eroders of Capital

The harsh reality is that bond investing requires every bit as much research and analysis as is needed in stock investing. Roger G. Ibbottson and Rex A. Sinquefield point out in their book, *Stocks, Bonds, Bills and Inflation. Historical Returns. (1926-1987)* (see Figure 4-2) that over a 60-year period of time, the bond market was a dismal performer. It only outperformed the stock market 25 times, or less than half the time. It gets worse if you factor in inflation and total performance over time. This eye-opening book also points out that $1 invested in Treasury-Bills in 1926 was worth $11.01 in 1991. If compared to $1 in stocks in 1926, the $1 was worth $675.59 in 1991.

In their annual Investor's Guide, *Fortune* magazine did a comparison of long-term government bonds, U.S. Treasury bills and stocks with inflation factored in. A mere $100

Figure 4-2 Wealth Indexes of Investments in U.S. Capital Markets (1926-1987) (Year-End 1925=1.00)

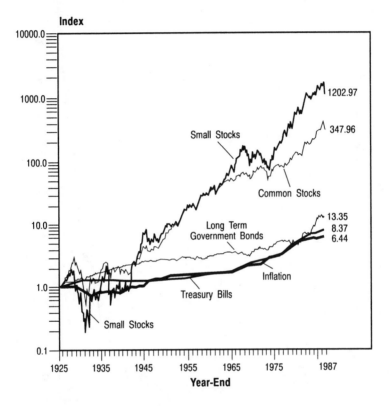

SOURCE: *Bonds, Bills and Inflation (SBBI), 1992 Yearbook,* Ibbotson Associates, Chicago.

invested in the stock market at the end of 1925, according to the graph, would be worth more than $50,000 today. The comparable figure for a $100 investment in T-Bills would be $942. Startling isn't it? (See Figure 4-3.)

Figure 4-3   The Compelling Case for Stocks

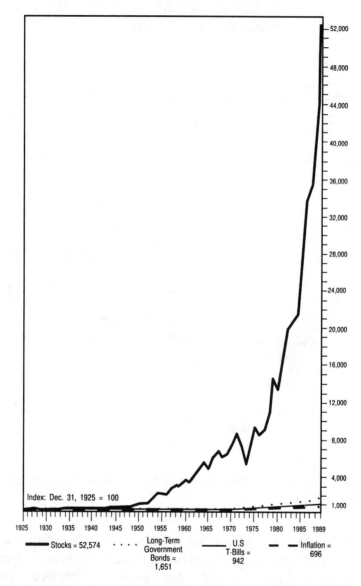

SOURCE: Ibbotson Associates, Chicago.

One more example from *Forbes* magazine, illustrates in a May 15, 1989 article the capital erosion from bond investing. The article covers performance of stocks versus bonds from 1946 to 1988. This includes the crash of October 1987. As you can see in Figure 4-4, a $10,000 investment in stocks, less inflation, is valued at $63,741. The same $10,000 in bonds is valued at $2,451.

And if you need more evidence, the actual fact book read by those studying to become certified financial analysts (CFA), *The Handbook of Fixed Income Securities,* by Frank J. Fabozzi and Irving M. Pollack, states in the first sentence of the first paragraph that "Although buy and hold is a realistic option for investors who buy equities, it is an act of wanton imprudence for investors in debt securities."

Figure 4-4   No Contest

Consider an investor who put $10,000 in the market (as measured by the S&P 500) in 1946 and another investor who put down ten times as much, $100,000 in long-term government bonds. Forty-three years later, after inflation and taxes, the stock investment would be worth more than $63,000, the bond position just under $25,000.

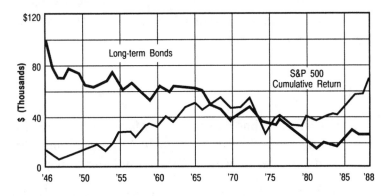

SOURCE: Dreman Value Management.

The experts and all of the historical data are trying to tell you something. The simple truth is that you have to view bonds as volatile instruments that paradoxically can be more risky than stocks. Look at what columnist Peter L. Bernstein says: "A lot of advisors say you should diversify your holdings between stocks and bonds. But experience says this advice is wrong. . . . The perception that bonds are less risky is insufficient justification for using them in a portfolio with stocks. . . . You can hold cash equivalents, which never have negative returns.[2] You must know what you are doing if you decide to buy bonds. You can't just sit on them and expect to make any money. They need to be traded like stocks. Just ask the institutional traders—they'll tell you it's a lot easier to be a "genius" in stocks than in bonds.

Bonds and Bacon—All Sizzle

Look, bonds are like bacon: it smells good, looks good, sounds good and tastes good. But eat enough of it and it will kill you. Just remember these two very important facts and you will avoid the headaches and heartaches of losing your hard-earned money on inappropriate investments:

Bonds are bad. And—when Wall Street meets Madison Avenue—you could lose.

Endnotes

[1] From exclusive book excerpt in *Money* (March 1993), "Beating the Street," by Peter Lynch. to be published by Simon and Schuster in March, 1993. © by Peter Lynch.

[2] From Peter L. Bernstein, "Who Needs Bonds?" *Forbes* (February 1, 1993).

5

A Dangerous Investment That Sounds Safe: Tax-Exempts

"[Prospectuses] are not designed to help investors, they are designed to disclose legal requirements."
— A. Michael Lipper, President
Lipper Analytical Services, Inc.

"But the simple truth is that you could print in huge red type across the prospectus, 'this investment is a real dog and will eat up all your hard-earned money and leave you destitute,' and investors would still buy the

fund . . . reason is most investors just don't read the prospectus."
—Walter L. Updegrave, Assoc. Ed
Money magazine[1]

You know the deal. If it looks like a duck, acts like a duck, and walks like a duck, it's a duck. When I talk about tax-exempt securities, I include municipal bonds (munies), municipal utility district bonds (M.U.D.s), tax-exempt trust units, tax-exempt mutual funds, and every other extraneous term Wall Street can dream up. But, as I always say: A bond is a bond is a bond.

In the early days of my business I became a real pro on the consequences of investing in bonds because I invested my own money in them! I sold championship amounts to the trusting public as I was "trained" to do by my firm. Now, when promotional bond literature arrives in my mail, I treat it like the junk mail I feel it really is by placing it in the round file under my desk. Since I took the time to read the fine print in the prospectus as they tell (but don't expect) me to do over and over in the promotional brochure, I already have the facts I need. It is a waste of time to sift through pictures of richly-appointed dens with blazing fireplaces and Grandma and Grandpa taking a stroll to the mailbox to pick up their interest checks. Why wade through flowery expressions about performance and double-talk about preservation of capital and safety when the real truth is spelled out in black and white in the prospectus (if you know how and where to find it).

That's why this chapter will become the most valuable body of information on investing you will ever read.

Read This, Then Pass It On to Your Broker

Let's talk about the "bait-and-switch" marketing tactics some companies use in their literature. Let's say I request a broker marketing kit from a bond fund company. The sales kit arrives in the most impressive marketing package you could imagine. It's very first class. The package includes a special booklet for me, the broker, which is very stately-looking, with full-color photographs depicting classy, traditional and sophisticated scenes. And believe me, it's all carefully thought out. The marketing folks understand the importance of making a good first impression. If a man is in one of the photos, you can bet he'll be grey or silver-haired (definitely not bald!). The woman in the photo will be the picture of loveliness and the epitome of motherhood. Photographs of homes and their interiors reek of wealth like something straight out of *Architectural Digest*. A simple gold-stamped title reads, "National Municipal Fund Shares." The tag line says, "Tax-Free Income for the High-Taxed Investor." The small print at the bottom explains, "For Dealer Use Only." Curious, isn't it?

Here is the first disclosure point. What the words, "For Dealer Use Only" do is protect the investment company—not the investor. The brochure is designed specifically to capture the broker's attention and divert his interest from other products he might wish to sell. The broker's kit is written in such a way that the broker is led to believe that the consumer really needs this product.

Let's analyze some statements, claims and data presentation in one of the brochures. On the cover is the headline, "The Growth and Appeal of Quality National Tax-Exempts." Right here—in the very beginning—the bait-and-switch is out in the open. All you have to do is re-read the headline. Note the word, "growth." It doesn't refer to the potential of the *investment*, but rather to the *growth of sales*. The bar graph from the brochure (Figure 5-1) adds bait to the impression, in a clever and subtle—yet legal—way that the investment product looks like it increases in value.

You now have a graph and some numbers that look no different than the earnings-per-share graphs all brokers are familiar with. It is important that it *appears* this way to brokers. Brokers are very used to reading corporate earnings

Figure 5-1   The Phenomenal Growth of Nirvanna Funds

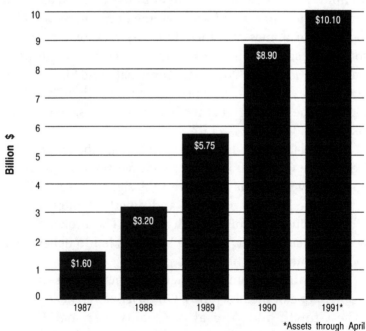

*Assets through April

*The past performance of Nirvanna Funds does not necessarily predict the future performance of these funds or the Income Fund.

figures. The more earnings a company has, the more the shares grow or increase in value. What broker *wouldn't* want to see corporate numbers showing this rate of growth? *But, these numbers are only depicting how many tax-exempt products this financial company is selling to the public.* In my opinion, this can be blatantly misleading and can create the wrong impression of this product.

Now, don't misunderstand. The graph does have its small print off to one side of the margin which reads, *"The past performance does not necessarily predict the future performance of these securities."* To protect themselves—and as required by law—the company includes the small print disclaimer as an attempt to avoid misconceptions in the minds of investors as a result of anything that might be implied or insinuated in the text. This is the sort of trick some lawyers use in court when they disclose information to the jury by "accident" and are reprimanded by the judge. The judge asks the jury to disregard what the lawyer said and has it stricken from the record. The lawyer proceeds (laughing to himself) and the damage has been done.

Consider some of the typical verbiage often used in reference to a portfolio philosophy of the brochure:

"... back-to-basics, *conservative* philosophy."

"... seeking *relative* safety."

"... ability to sift complex markets *seeking* performance."

"... .*expects t*o purchase the top categories."

"... maintaining *relative safety.*"

"... *Initial Anticipated Structure.* 20% AAA, 20%AA, 35%A and 25%BAA."

"... management choice is for today's intelligent investor and for tomorrow's."

And there's more:

> "... designed to respond to today's complex affairs."
> "... attractive monthly dividends, tax-free."
> "... stability, New York Stock Exchange listing and management from a company in the business since 1940."

Read all of the above very carefully. You will notice that every word is vague, hedged, grandiose. The claims have no substance. Here's why:

Conservative—This word is used by everyone. Everyone thinks they are conservative.

Relative—Relative to what? Bonds were more volatile than stocks in the 80s.

Seeking—Being able and getting the job done is one thing, but seeking is the same as trying or hoping. There is no conviction in the word "seeking." The same goes for the word "expect." If the investment loses money, what redeeming value is there to words like "seeking," "expects," and even "relative safety"?

Look at the words "Anticipated Initial Structure" on the top categories allocation. Twenty percent went to AAA bonds, but a greater percentage was allocated to BAA. Also notice that this is the "initial" structure. This is a key word. It means what it says. Does this mean that, later, 80 percent could go to BAA bonds?

Aha! Here's the Bait

Because it is tax-free, other investments would have to earn more to pay the 28 or 31 percent tax. For example, the tax equivalent to a 70 percent tax-free bond is 9.72 if you are in the 28 percent bracket. If you are in a higher bracket, you would have to get even more yield.

And what does the small print say? "This data is for illustrating only and is not intended to predict actual fund yields."

> **" R**ead all of the material very carefully. You will notice that every word is vague, hedged, grandiose. The claims have no substance."

Why the small print, you say? Could it be the yields reflected are not achieved? Exactly. They don't want to legally imply you could expect, for example, 7 percent every year on your investment value. Furthermore, the taxable equivalent is based on the 28 percent and 31 percent tax bracket that may or may not be understood correctly. That is up to you or your tax expert.

If you are reporting earnings of $100,000 from your and your wife's combined salaries, you are supposedly in the 28 and 31 percent tax brackets. Does that mean if you earn 7 percent in dividends they will be taxed at 28 or 31 percent? Not necessarily. You and your wife probably have a mortgage, donate to charity, and have some capital investment losses from some bond swap last year. Your net adjusted income after your deductions might bring your taxable income level down to $30,000. If so, your 7 percent tax-exempt dividends have far fewer tax advantages since your adjusted tax bracket might be down to 15-20 percent.

The taxable equivalent tables using the convenient high tax brackets of 28 and 31 percent are great if your adjusted net income after deductions is up there at $100,000. What if you earned $350,000, but had $360,000 in deductions! You'd pay no taxes, and might even apply for welfare.

Here's the Switch

Now, tax-exempt income is compared to certificates of deposit income. The message is that in order to obtain the same after-tax income, it takes fewer dollars invested in tax-exempts than in CDs. Forget trying to keep up with the mathematics. What's important to understand is that the marketing material has you comparing the risk investment of tax-exempts to the risk-free investment of CDs in their terms for legal purposes. What you are now comparing are apples to Jalepenos!

Note the small print:

> *"This data is for discussion purposes and is not actual results. Certificates are short-term investments insured by a federal government department which pays established fixed principal and interest. The tax-exempt is a long-term investment with a changing yield and market value."*

Remember earlier, they did not want to legally imply that 7 percent was a constant and level earnings each year. To cover the complexity, the last line of the small print says, *"See 'Footnotes to data' for important additional information."* This is a confusing statement since it is not easily understood which footnotes they are referring to. Plus, if the information is *that* valuable and important, why on earth is it in a footnote? Hmmm.

The implication is that by investing in this product we have a conservative, higher-paying, better-than-a-CD investment for ourselves. Using glib verbiage and hedging in small print, nothing legal supports those claims or impressions. Also, did you happen to catch in the last small print, the words, ". . . fluctuating tax-free rates and market value?" What are they talking about? You thought this investment was like a CD? Well, you came to that conclusion because it was *implied by them* and that's what they want you to think.

Next, the brochure explains how you can protect your income. Wait a minute—why do you have to do that? You probably thought this was a conservative product sold by the largest, oldest tax-exempt company around! So, what happened to the *attractive, stable* and *experienced management* of a company 300 years old? Something to think about, right?

That Pesky Asterisk

On the subject of protecting your income, the marketing brochure proceeds to graph the risk of short-term investing over long-term investing. The graph explains that in the past couple of years, if you bought the tax-exempt fund, you would have locked in a 10.25 percent* yield for that same period of time. If, instead, you had bought CDs, you would have only received 9.5 percent, and interest rates over the past few years have fallen and your CDs would have paid you less on each renewal date.

Well, isn't 10.25 percent* locked long-term better than 9.5 percent short-term? No, not necessarily. Remember, the

10.25 percent* has that asterisk* beside it all the time. Why? Very simple. It is really not 10.25 percent. That asterisk is there to remind you that in the small print it is explained as the *taxable equivalent.* The actual interest for a 30 percent tax bracket is 7.17 percent. If your actual, effective adjusted tax bracket is less than 25 percent, you would be better off with a 9.5 percent CD!

Furthermore, the graph makes no mention of the fact that if, for the past few years, you had locked in a 9.5 percent, 10-year CD, as interest rates fell, you still would have earned the same high 9.5 percent rate, not the lower 6.5 percent rate implied.

Am I being too zealous in the critique and analysis of this product? Are you still skeptical? Note again the small print disclaimer provided by the securities firm brochure, *"The past performance does not predict future earnings. Short-term investments like CDs and long-term investments like National Trust Tax-Exempts each have distinctive factors. The tax-exempts may fluctuate with market conditions and fluctuate even more due to additional investment strategies available to the manager of these bond funds. See the 'Strategies' section in the prospectus."*

Whoa! What's going on here, you say? The tax-exempts are not like CDs and the fund managers can use strategies other than conservative top investment tax-exempt bonds?

You bet they can. *And it can either improve or damage the portfolio results!* No disclosure of other risk elements have been introduced, no explanation, unless you read the *prospectus.*

So pick your poison. Now the brochure attempts to address the value of tax-exempts currently and for the long-term.

More Bait

"...The best way to compare the tax-exempt with other alternatives is by using a level playing field using bottom-line, after-tax returns." In the following table, the comparison numbers show these results assuming a 20% effective tax rate:

Investment	Yield	Net after-tax total return
High-yield fund	14.2%	11.36%
US Govt Fund Avg	8.10	6.48
Jumbo CD	9.50	7.60
Tax-exempt	7.10	7.10

More Switch

Here's where the numbers game is played: What if you bought the most speculative of the alternatives—the high-yield fund. These are, in reality, the junk bond funds of the 80s. It's not a fair comparison since junk bond investing is done by speculators, not conservative investors. However, let's say you bought the 14.2 percent high-yield fund as an investment and didn't worry about selling it to establish a total return scenario. You would have earned the 14.2 percent and, even if you paid the highest tax at the correct net adjusted tax rate of 30 percent, even then your return would be 70 percent of 14.2, or 9.94 percent.

Let's assume you bought government bond funds because you didn't have much money and you wanted to have something very safe. If you have a low income, you are probably in a low tax bracket as well. What if you received 8.10 percent and only paid a 10 percent effective tax. You would have earned 7.29 percent after tax plus the after tax capital gain of 5.52 percent (interest rates came down and you sold) to establish the level bottom line return of 12.81 percent. Now that's better than the boasting of 10.25* of the riskier tax-exempt funds. Keep in mind the reason for the asterisk is to disclose that this return of 10.25* is a taxable equivalent at a 30% tax rate, the real coupon yield of the tax exempt fund is only 7.17%. Now the government bond fund of 12.81 percent after tax is substantially better. What you need to realize is that there are different reasons for buying different investments, therefore there is little value in comparing all investments on a "level playing field."

Are you still skeptical? Just look at the small print again. "*The past performance does not predict future performance. The investments compared here represent a varied array of fixed yielding investment alternatives, each with different features. See 'Additional data of graphs information.'*"

And what is even more subtle, again, is the comparison of various risk investments such as high-yield junk bonds, government bonds, tax-exempt bonds, to the risk-free CD. This is not an accident. It's called effective marketing—at your expense. To compare the risky tax-exempts to CDs as often as possible to establish in your mind, as a fact, that all investments are comparable is very shrewd. In fact, in the graph, the CD bar is next to the tax-exempt bar. This is like rubbing elbows with some VIP. Remember the various bond investments are like Jalepeno peppers, not like apples. The CD is the apple.

It's All Done with Mirrors

Now the brochure performs one of my "favorite" tricks of the trade. The marketing guide describes the long-term performance of the investment. This device establishes the impression of profitability to the reader by illustrating the "Premium to Net Asset Value" history. This is a very creative move.

This particular graph shows how often the value of the investment traded for more than the cash value or book value of the portfolio by market factors such as demand and dealer mark-ups. Obviously, there is a line that shows that almost all the time the value of the investment is greater than the value of the portfolio. In fact, 77 percent of the time it was higher.

But, what does premium to net asset value really mean? Does it mean the investment by the consumer had a profit 77 percent of the time? No.

Let me explain. Let's say you bought this investment at $10.50. The portfolio value or book value was $10. Because of the demand, the dealer mark-up or profit to sell to the demanding buyer was $.50. This means the tax-exempt fund is trading at $.50 over book value, or a premium to net asset value. Now let's say the demand or dealer commission stayed at $.50 over the net asset value over a period of time when interest rates went up continuously. When interest rates go up, the value of bonds go down continuously as well. Therefore, the net asset value of the bonds goes down steadily. As a result, you could find yourself owning this investment down to $4.50, showing a continuous loss on your investment from $10.50 to $4.50. That represents a 57 percent loss. Yet, at $4.50, remember the portfolio and net asset value is $4, and the premium of $.50 is still there. This means that 100 percent of the time you had a "premium to net asset value" and yet 100 percent of the time you were losing money. In fact, a loss of 57 percent!

I see no value or merit to the term "premium to net asset value." It's really very close to misleading information. It is legal, though, because it's technically correct data. However, you have to wonder if the broker selling the stuff really understands it. Hopefully, the broker will comply with the small print: *"Dealer information only." This memorandum relates to a public offering. Under no circumstances may a copy of this information be shown or given to any member of the public. All reps should read the preliminary prospectus before discussing the offering with potential investors. "*

The marketing brochure says that the portfolio managers stress long-term performance and will protect the future dividend by investing in 7- to 10-year bonds with protection. It sounds good. But it doesn't matter if one really understands what that means. The point to have covered is that the managers have the investment covered for the next 10 years.

However, bonds regularly are bought with 20- or 30-year maturities. These "longer bonds" pay a much higher dividend and can enhance the yield today to look better in comparison to current alternative products. *These longer-term bonds have substantially more market risk.*

The marketing brochure addresses this key area, which is the most crucial to performance and the most difficult, by bringing it up like this: *"The longer bond prices can fluctuate more due to changing market factors. The portfolio managers may invest in leveraged strategies or issue separate classes of shares. See 'special leverage factors' in the prospectus. "*

That's all folks. Nothing more on the most difficult and crucial variables that historically have caused the tax-exempt bond market to perform poorly.

Good. You Can Still Trade for Less

If all of that information was vague to you when you pre-viously invested in a bond fund, don't worry. The marketing data mentions that you can get out anytime (you probably read that in your own brochure). So the great liquidity factor is discussed now. The tax-exempt securities can be traded because they are listed on the New York Stock Exchange. One sentence reads something like this:

"Like all securities that trade, the prices will fluctuate with market factors and at the time of trading may be worth more or less than the cost of your investment."

Wait a minute! Trading for *less* than the cost? That's a loss! (Now are you getting the picture?)

This disclosure is the last to be made in the portfolio strategy section. After several paragraphs of sophisticated comments on 10-year or shorter-term bonds and special trading techniques for longer-term, 20- to 30-year bonds, a simple statement mentions that you could lose on the in-vestment. That again, I maintain, is to protect the packagers of the investment—not the investor.

No one likes to bother reading the small print. The marketers know that. The regulators, however, have done their job and require full disclosure. The securities compa-nies really do want to comply with all regulations. So, they do make all disclosures.

Need More Proof?

If you think the opinions expressed in this chapter about tax-exempt securities are overly-biased, or slanted, or too harsh, look at Figure 5-2, what I consider to be a classic

Figure 5-2   Full Disclosure

Generate the Same After-Tax Income

This chart is for illustrative purposes only and is not intended to predict actual Fund yields. The 6-month Jumbo CD rate shown here is representative of rates generally, as reported in the *The Wall Street Journal*. It is not intended to represent the return available from any specific investment. CDs are insured to $100,000 by an agency of the federal government; they are taxable, short-term investments that pay fixed principal and interest but are subject to fluctuating rollover rates. The municipal fund is not insured, and is a long-term investment with a fluctuating yield and market value.

The Risk of Using Short-Term Investments for Long-Term Money

The fund average shows, for a given point in time, the composite taxable equivalent yield available to an investor in the federal 31% tax bracket using each of the national exchange-traded funds that were in existence and had commenced paying dividends at the time. This average does not necessarily predict the future yields of these funds and has no necessary relationship to the future yield of the municipal fund. Several of these funds have different investment objectives and capital structures than the municipal fund. The municipal fund's yield will depend on many factors, including yields on the bonds purchased for its portfolio, operating expenses and the rate paid on its preferred stock after issuance.

As noted above, CDs are insured to $100,000 by an agency of the federal government. They are taxable, short-term investments that pay a fixed principal and interest but are subject to fluctuating rollover rates. The money market fund average shown represents uninsured, taxable investments with a fixed net asset value, special features facilitating liquidity and a fluctuating yield. The municipal fund is not insured, and is a long-term investment with a fluctuating yield and market value.

The Opportunity for Enhanced Income

U.S. Treasury securities are generally subject to less volatility than municipal bonds from credit concerns, due primarily to the fact that the timely payment of principal and interest is backed by the full faith and credit of the U.S. Government.

Consider Taxable Equivalent Yields and Total Returns

All current market yields shown are based on data as of March 31, 1991. The fund average taxable equivalent yield and taxable equivalent total return figures are based on the 31% federal tax rate. All total return figures shown are based on net asset value and are for the one-year period ending March 31, 1991. Total returns based on net asset value do not take sales charges or underwriting concessions into account, and for exchange-traded funds may differ from total return based on market price.

The average yield for funds uses annualized dividends and market prices as of March 31, 1991, for the national funds that were in existence and had commenced paying dividends for the entire preceding year. The fund average taxable equivalent total return has been computed by assuming a 32% tax rate for these same funds. Various total returns on net asset value over this period for the funds used in constructing this average. The past performance of the funds shown does not predict their future results, nor does the past performance of these funds predict the future results of the municipal fund. Several of these funds have different investment objectives than the municipal fund.

The averages shown are based on categories of open-end funds. Unlike open-end funds, closed-end funds share prices trade at a market value which may be above or below net asset value.

Figure 5-2   Full Disclosure (continued)

The Jumbo CD data was compiled from Federal Reserve statistics showing average yields for $100,000 6-mo. CDs for the week of March 31, 1990, of 8.52% and for the week of September 30, 1990, of 8.06%.

The taxable equivalent total return of a tax-free fund represents the total return that would be generated by a taxable income fund that produced the same amount of after-tax income and change in net asset value as the tax-free fund in each year, assuming the specified tax rate. A comparison of taxable equivalent total return of a tax-free fund to the total return of a taxable fund may facilitate a comparison of the funds' investment performance distributions are taken into account.

Comparison with other long-term funds of long-term funds shown here, because of the character of their underlying securities, may differ from municipal bond funds in several respects. The susceptibility of investment-grade corporate bonds and municipal bonds to market interest rate changes and general credit changes is similar. High current yield corporate bonds are subject to a greater degree of volatility resulting from changes in market interest rates than municipal bonds and are particularly susceptible to volatility from credit changes. U.S. Treasury securities are generally subject to less volatility from credit concerns than municipal bonds, due primarily to the fact that the timely pay-ment of principal and interest is backed by the full faith and credit of the U.S. Government.

Comparisons with short-term investments
As noted earlier, CDs are short-term instruments whose rates reflect market conditions at the time of purchase. CD principal and interest payments are insured up to $100,000 by an agency of the federal government. For these reasons, CDs are not subject to price volatility from either general credit changes or from changes in market interest rates, and accordingly provide the benefit of preservation of principal. Money market funds are uninsured investments offering stable net asset value, special features facilitating liquidity and daily fluctuating yields. Because CDs and money market funds are short-term in nature, they represent different types of investments than the others shown here, including the funds, which are all long-term investments whose value will tend to fluctuate with market interest rates.

Trading at a Premium to Net Asset Value
The price and net asset value histories of funds used in this composite do not necessarily predict the future price or net asset value performance of those funds or of the municipal fund. Several of these funds have different investment objectives and capital structures than the municipal fund.

disclosure made in a typical successful marketing brochure that is just for "Dealer Information Only."

There it is in full disclosure form. Keep in mind this format is still just for the "dealers." Throughout the brochure and especially towards the end, the dealers are reminded that they can't use this brochure for the public. They must, by law, give the investor the prospectus. That's why all the consumer marketing data says: *"For more information read the prospectus before making an investment."*

You see, the prospectus is not a marketing device. It is the Securities Exchange Commission solution to a long-standing problem of protecting the investors from sales hype, over-zealous marketing, and misleading information.

Why is all this protection needed for the investment consumer? Before showing aspects disclosed in the prospectus, let's examine a specific set of numbers. These should say something to you. They do to me. For serious investing over three-year periods or longer, tax-exempts don't give a net after-tax return worth investing in, especially for the risk.

Table 5-1 is an actual client record of investing a total of $166,248.96 over a period from May 29, 1979 to April 20, 1989. The client ended with $183,016.25 (44,421.42 × 4.12). Nothing was taken out during that time. Over the 10-year period, the client made $16,767.29 or 10.08% in 10 years, or about 1% per year!

Another actual account we can look at (Figure 5-3) was that of a client who was told by the sales representative that the tax-exempt fund was as safe as a CD. She, of course, believed him and didn't read the prospectus. On January 1, 1987 the share value was $10.14. By October 30, it was $9.41. That was a 7 percent loss in 10 months.

The information is all around you. Check out the sales presentation. A good advisor won't mind and will want you to because his data should prove to be accurate after you do your research.

When all else fails, read the directions. Better yet, when all else fails, read the prospectus. The regulators have done their job by the requirement to disclose. The investment companies have done their job by providing you with a

Table 5-1   Tax-Exempt Bond Fund

Date Purchased	Shares	Total Shares	Average Cost/ Share	Cost	Total Cost
5/29/1979	3,017.727	3,017.727	$4.68	$14,129.00	$14,129.00
DIV.1979	113.405	3,131.132	4.42	501.77	14,630.77
DIV.1980	265.027	3,396.159	3.63	961.89	15,592.66
DIV.1981	365.388	3,761.547	2.97	1,084.58	16,677.24
DIV.1982	1,240.317	5,001.864	3.07	3,812.41	20,489.65
3/23/1982	10,416.667	15,418.531	2.88	30,000.00	50,489.65
DIV.1983	1,422.423	16,840.954	3.48	4,947.26	55,436.91
DIV.1984	1,609.247	18,450.201	3.37	5,424.51	60,862.42
DIV.1985	1,678.123	20,128.324	3.59	5,030.57	66,892.99
DIV.1986	1,527.608	21,655.930	4.09	6,253.41	73,146.40
DIV.1987	1,646.080	23,302.010	3.98	6,548.96	79,695.36
DIV.1988	1,722.454	25,024.464	3.96	6,820.07	86,515.43
1/1/1989*	151.453	25,175.917	4.00	605.66	87,121.09
2/27/1989	4,850.598	30,026.515	4.12	20,000.00	107,121.09
2/1/1989*	152.983	30,179.498	3.95	604.13	107,725.22
3/13/1989	4,893.708	35,073.206	4.11	20,115.18	127,840.40
3/13/1989	5,374.660	40,447.866	4.11	22,092.09	149,932.49
3/1989*	221.022	40,668.888	3.91	864.64	150,797.13
4/20/1989	3,752.532	44,421.420	4.12	15,451.83	166,248.96

*Monthly dividends reinvested.

prospectus. The sales representative has done his job by giving you a prospectus. Now you do your job. It's your money. Read the prospectus. I can't stress this enough.

OK, you don't want to read all of it. Well, the least you can do is read the parts about cost, risk, market value, and performance. Find those parts and study them.

Figure 5-3   Summary of Your Account

SUMMARY OF YOUR ACCOUNT

STATEMENT DATE	INCOME DIVIDENDS PAID THIS YEAR	CAPITAL GAINS PAID THIS YEAR	CERTIFICATE SHARES HELD BY YOU	+	UNISSUED SHARES	=	TOTAL SHARES YOU OWN
/01/87	301.56	.00	.00	+	531.065	=	531.065

BUTIONS ARE: DIVIDEND DISTRIBUTION   REINVEST   CAPITAL GAIN DISTRIBUTION   REINVEST

RECENT TRANSACTIONS

OF ACTION	TYPE OF TRANSACTION	DOLLAR AMOUNT	PRICE PER SHARE	SHARES THIS TRANSACTION	TOTAL SHARES
	BEGINNING BALANCE				475.953
1 01 87	INCOME DIVIDEND	25.62	10.14	2.527	478.480
2 30 87	INCOME DIVIDEND	26.32	10.17	2.588	481.068
2 27 87	INCOME DIVIDEND	26.46	10.22	2.589	483.657
3 31 87	INCOME DIVIDEND	26.60	10.33	2.575	486.232
4 30 87	INCOME DIVIDEND	26.74	9.72	2.751	488.983
5 28 87	INCOME DIVIDEND	26.89	9.65	2.787	491.770
5 31 87	INT IMIT 053 0000179694	230.00	9.89	23.256	515.026
6 28 87	PRN IMIT 053 0000179694	11.35	9.89	1.148	516.174
6 28 87	INCOME DIVIDEND	27.76	9.73	2.853	519.027
7 31 87	INCOME DIVIDEND	28.55	9.76	2.925	521.952
3 31 87	INCOME DIVIDEND	28.71	9.78	2.936	524.888
3 30 87	INCOME DIVIDEND	28.87	9.34	3.091	527.979
0 30 87	INCOME DIVIDEND	29.04	9.41	3.086	531.065

Dissecting a Live One—Not for the Squeamish

Let me extract portions of a typical tax-exempt fund prospectus from one of the larger marketers of bond funds (Figure 5-4). Take care to notice the underscored portions and how they differ in description from the "Dealer Only" marketing kit.

Do you see the vague words? *"Objective." "Opinion." "Will seek." "Intends." "It is anticipated."*

Notice right on the front page it says: *"All or a portion of the fund's dividends may be subject to the Federal Alternative Minimum Tax."* This means tax-free may not be tax-free.

Also notice *"special risks"* are disclosed.

Look at the Table of Contents (Figure 5-5).

There is no section discussing "risk." No chapter on cost. But if you read "Special Leverage Considerations," "Certain Trading Strategies," "Net Asset Value," and "Tax Matters" you will find it all disclosed.

The investment objectives (Figure 5-6) are vague and hedged, but they bring up the fact that you could experience losses and a declining market.

Let's take a look at these specific investments. And you thought they were safe!

Figure 5-7 clearly states that the fund not only has risk, but an increase of risk due to *leveraging* up commodity futures and options.

Tax-frees can be taxable, as shown in Figure 5-8.

Again, risk in the marketplace and even greater risk with leverage strategies. Some risk factors are "beyond the control" of the fund manager.

Basically, as shown in Figure 5-9, you can say if you have too high a tax bracket, you may not get any tax advantage by owning tax-exempt securities. The reciprocal is also true. If your bracket is too low, you lose the tax advantage

Figure 5-4   Sample Prospectus

Common Stock

ABC Fund (hereafter referred to as "the Fund") is a newly organized, closed-end, diversified management investment company. ABC's primary investment objective is current income exempt from regular Federal income tax, and its secondary investment objective is the enhancement of portfolio value relative to the municipal bond market through investments in tax-exempt municipal obligations (as defined herein) that, in the opinion of ABC's investment adviser, are underrated or under-valued or that represent municipal market sectors that are undervalued. ABC will seek to achieve its investment objectives by investing substantially all of its assets in a diversified portfolio of tax-exempt municipal obligations rated within the four highest grades (Baa or BBB or better), except that up to 20% of ABC's assets may be invested in unrated municipal obligations which, in the opinion of ABC's invest-ment adviser, are of comparable quality to those so rated. See "Investment Objectives and Policies" No assurances can be given that ABC's investment objectives will be achieved. All or a portion of ABC's dividends may be subject to the Federal alternative minimum tax. Investors are advised to read this Prospectus and retain it for future reference.

Approximately three to six months after completion of the offering of Common Stock described herein, ABC intends to offer shares of preferred stock representing approximately 35% of ABC's capital immediately after the time the preferred stock is issued. The issuance of preferred stock will result in the financial leveraging of the Common Stock. Although the timing and other terms of the preferred stock offering and the terms of the preferred stock will be determined by ABC's Board of Directors, it is anticipated that the preferred stock will pay dividends based on short-term rates, and that the proceeds of the preferred stock offering will be invested at long-term rates. Investors should note that there are special risks associated with the leveraging of the Common Stock. See "Special Leverage Considerations" and "Description of Capital Stock."

Prior to this offering, there has been no public market for the Common Stock. The Common Stock has been approved for listing on the New York Stock Exchange, subject to official notice of issuance.

THESE SECURITIES HAVE NOT BEEN APPROVED OR DISAPPROVED BY THE SECURITIES AND EXCHANGE COMMISSION OR ANY STATE SECURITIES COMMISSION NOR HAS THE SECURITIES AND EXCHANGE COMMISSION OR ANY STATE SECURITIES COMMISSION PASSED UPON THE ACCURACY OR ADEQUACY OF THIS PROSPECTUS. ANY REPRESENTATION TO THE CON-TRARY IS A CRIMINAL OFFENSE.

Figure 5-5   Table of Contents

of tax-free securities. You are on your own, because the prospectus says to consult your tax expert, not them.

The prospectus clearly states the portfolio will "emphasize" long-term maturities. They have the most risk:

Figure 5-6   Prospectus Investment Objectives

Investment Objectives ...

The <u>primary</u> investment objective of ABC is <u>current income</u> exempt from regular Federal income tax. The <u>secondary</u> investment objective of ABC is the <u>enhancement of portfolio value relative to the municipal bond market</u> through investments in tax-exempt bonds that, in the opinion of ABC's investment adviser, are underrated or undervalued or that represent municipal market sectors that are undervalued. By purchasing such tax-exempt bonds, ABC <u>will seek</u> to realize above-average <u>capital appreciation in a rising market and to experience less than average capital losses in a declining market.</u> Except as described below, ABC will seek to achieve its investment objectives by investing substantially all of its assets in tax-exempt Municipal Obligations rated at the time of purchase within the four highest grades (Baa or BBB or better) by Moody's or S&P, <u>except that up to 20% of ABC's assets may be invested in unrated Municipal</u> Obligation which, in the opinion of ABC's investment adviser, have credit characteristics equivalent to, and are of comparable quality to, Municipal Obligations which are so rated. During <u>temporary defensive periods</u> and in order to keep cash on hand fully invested, ABC may invest in high quality, short-term tax-exempt and taxable temporary investments.

The Fund intends to emphasize investments in municipal obligations with long-term maturities in order to maintain an average portfolio maturity of 20-30 years, but the average maturity may be shortened from time to time depending on market conditions. As a result, the Fund's portfolio at any given time may include both long-term and intermediate-term municipal obligations. Moreover,

The top three safety categories, by the rating services "are not absolute standards of quality." Safety is disclosed above, as are other variables of risk:

The yields on municipal obligations are dependent on a variety of factors, including the condition of the general money market and the municipal obligation market, the size of a particular offering, the maturity of the obligation and the rating of the issue. The ratings of Moody's and S&P represent their opinions as to the quality of those municipal obligations that they rate. It should be emphasized, however, that ratings are general and are not absolute standards of quality.

Figure 5-7

No assurances?

There can be no assurance that the Fund's investment objectives will be achieved. See "investment Objectives and Policies." In seeking to achieve its investment objectives, the Fund may employ certain trading strategies such as purchasing securities on a when-issued or delayed delivery basis and engaging in financial futures and options transactions, subject to certain restrictions. See "Certain Trading Strategies of the Fund."

Futures? Commodities? Options?

. . . operating expenses, the effect of leverage will be to cause Common Shareholders to realize a higher current rate of return than if the Fund were not leveraged. However, if the current dividend rate on the preferred stock were to approach the net return on the Fund's investment portfolio after expenses, the benefit of leverage to Common Shareholders would be reduced, and if the current dividend rate on the preferred stock were to exceed the net return on the Fund's portfolio, the Fund's leveraged capital structure would result in a lower rate of return to the Common Shareholders.

Lower rate of return

ers. Similarly, since any net capital appreciaiton in the Fund's assets generally would be relected in an increase in the net asset value attributable to the Fund's Common Stock, if there is an increase in the net asset value of the Fund's investment portfolio the effect of leverage would be to increase the net asset value per share of Common Stock to a greater extent than if the Fund were not leveraged. On the other hand, since any decline in the net asset value of the Fund's investment

Decline in the net asset value

Declining market mentioned again and even greater decline in net asset value.

portfolio is borne entirely by Common Shareholders, the effect of leverage in a declining market would be to cause a greater decline in the net asset value of the Common Stock than if the Fund were not leveraged, which would likely be reflected in a greater decline in the market price for shares of Common Stock. Reflecting the foregoing, leverage creates risks for Common Shareholders, including the likelihood of greater volatility of the net asset value and market value of shares of Common Stock, and the risk that fluctuations in the short-term dividend rates of the preferred stock may affect the yield to Common shareholders. *See*

Leverage, greater volatility, risk that fluctuates

Figure 5-7   (continued)

If any?

"Special Leverage Considerations." Once the preferred stock is issued, Common Shareholders will
receive any net income of the Fund remaining after
payment of cumulative dividends on preferred
stock, and will receive at least annual distributions
of net capital gains, if any, to the extent not necessary to satisfy the dividend, redemption or . . .

Figure 5-8

. . . not ordinarily be a suitable investment for investors who are subject to the Federal alternative minimum tax. The suitability of shares of Common Stock
for these investors will depend upon a comparison
of the yield likely to be provided from the Fund with
the yield from comparable tax-exempt investments
not subject to the Federal alternative minimum tax,
and with the yield from comparable fully taxable
investments, in light of each such investor's tax
position. See "Tax Matters."

All costs are borne by the investors. Even if the investors sue the advisor and management, their legal costs are
paid by the investors:

All fees and expenses are accrued daily and deducted before payment of dividends
to investors.

In addition to the fee of the Adviser, the Fund pays all
other costs and expenses of its operations including compensation of its directors (other than those affiliated with
the Adviser), custodian, transfer and dividend disbursing

Figure 5-9

Tax-frees can be taxable

. . . liquidation preferences of the <u>Federal alternative minimum tax, the Fund would not</u> ordinarily be a suitable investment for investors who are subject to the <u>Federal alternative minimum tax.</u> See "Tax Matters."

Market Price of Shares

Shares of municipal closed-end fixed-income investment companies such as the Fund <u>may trade either at a discount to</u> or premium <u>over net asset value,</u> including during the period immediately after the commencement of a fund's initial public offering. <u>Net asset value generally increases when interest rates decline, and</u> decreases when interest rates rise, <u>and these changes are likely to be greater in the case of a fund having a leveraged capital structure. Whether investors will realize gains or losses upon the sale of shares of common Stock will not depend upon the Fund's net asset value but will depend entirely upon whether the market price of the Common Stock at the time of sale is above or below the original purchase price for the shares. Since the market price of the Fund's shares of Common Stock will be determined by such factors as relative demand for and supply of such shares in the market, general market and economic conditions and other factors beyond the control of the Fund, the Fund cannot predict whether shares of the Common Stock will trade at, below or above net asset value.</u> Accordingly, shares of the Common Stock are designed primarily for long-term investors, and investors in the Common Stock should not view the Fund as a vehicle for trading purposes. See "Special Leverage Consideration," "Net Asset Value" and "Repurchase of Fund Shares; Conversion to Open-End Fund."

expenses, legal fees, expenses of independent accountants, expenses of repurchasing shares, expenses of preparing, printing and distributing shareholder reports, notices, proxy statements and reports to governmental agencies, and taxes, if any.

Can you find where in this section it discusses that the net asset value at the time of selling could be below what you paid?

The net asset value of shares of the Fund's Common Stock will be determined by MBA Bank of Chicago, the Fund's custodian, as of 4:00 P.M. Eastern Time on the last day of each week on which the New York Stock Exchange, Inc. (the "Exchange") is open for trading, or at such other time or times as the Adviser deems appropriate. As of the date of this Prospectus, the Exchange is not open for trading on New Year's Day, Presidents' Day, Good Friday, Memorial Day, Independence Day, Labor Day, Thanksgiving Day and Christmas Day. The net asset value per share of Common Stock will be computed by dividing the value of the Fund's total assets, less liabilities and less the liquidation value of any outstanding shares of the Fund's preferred stock (expected to equal the original purchase price per share plus any accrued and unpaid dividends thereon, whether or not earned or declared), by the number of shares of Common Stock outstanding.

In determining net asset value for the Fund, the Fund's custodian utilizes the valuations of portfolio securities at the mean between the quoted bid and asked price or the yield equivalent when quotations are readily available. Securities for which quotations are not readily available (which will constitute a majority of the securities held by the Fund) are valued at fair value as determined by the pricing service using methods which include consideration of: yields or prices to value from dealers; and general market conditions. The pricing service may employ electronic data processing techniques or a matrix system, or both, to determine valuations. The procedures of the pricing service and its valuations are reviewed by the officers of the Fund under the general supervision of the Board of Directors.

Shares of municipal closed-end, fixed-income investment companies may trade either at a discount to or premium over net asset value. Net asset value generally increases when interest rates decline, and decreases when interest rates rise, and these changes are likely to be greater in the case of a fund having a leveraged capital structure. Since the market price of shares of the Fund's Common Stock will be determined by factors including relative demand for a supply of such shares in the market, general market and economic conditions and other factors beyond the control of the Fund, the Fund cannot predict whether shares of Common stock will trade at, below, or above net asset value. See "Special Leverage Considerations" and "Repurchase of Fund Shares; Conversion to Open-End Fund."

Here we do see the possibility of a loss to the investor. This line has to do with capital gain or loss treatment for tax purposes. Nonetheless, you could have a loss:

The sale or other disposition of Fund shares will normally result in capital gain or loss to shareholders. Generally a shareholder's gain or loss will be a long-term gain or loss if the shares have been held for more than one year. Present law taxes both long- and short-term capital gains of corporations at the rates applicable to ordinary income.

More possible taxes on your tax-free investment:

State and Local Tax Matters

The exemption from Federal income tax for exempt-interest dividends does not necessarily result in exemption for such dividends under the income or other tax laws of any state or local taxing authority. Some states exempt from state income tax that portion of any exempt-interest dividend that is derived from interest received by a regulated investment company on its holdings of securities of that state and its political subdivisions and instrumentalities. Therefore, the Fund will report annually to its shareholders the percentage of interest income earned by the Fund during the preceding year on tax-exempt obligations indicating, on a state-by-state basis, the source of such income. Shareholders of the Fund are advised to consult with their own tax advisers about state and local tax matters.

The following disclaimer is really saying that all the information provided to the brokers promoting kits cannot be used unless it is also in the prospectus. It also protects the issuers of the prospectus from any over-zealous sales representatives. If misrepresentations are made, the company is protected by disciplining the rep:

No dealer, salesman or other person has been authorized to give any information or to make any representation not contained in this Prospectus and, if given or made, such information or representation must not be relied upon as having been authorized by the Fund or any Underwriter. This Prospectus does not constitute an offer to sell or a solicitation of an offer to buy any of the securities offered hereby in any jurisdiction to any person to whom it is unlawful to make such offer in such jurisdiction.

The question might be, how is the broker-dealer going to remember what the "first-class, promotional broker-dealer brochure" teaches versus what the "prospectus on cheap paper" says in the small print?

You can even get more information. Talk about full disclosure! It's all here if you make the effort:

Additional Information

A Registration Statement on Form N-2, including amendments thereto, relating to the shares offered hereby, has been filed by the Fund with the Securities and Exchange Commission (the "Commission"), Washington, D.C. This Prospectus does not contain all of the information set forth in the Registration Statement, including any exhibits and schedules thereto. For further information with respect to the Fund and the shares offered hereby, reference is made to the Registration Statement. Statements contained in this Prospectus as to the contents of any contract or other document referred to are not necessarily complete and in each instance reference is made to the copy of such contract or other document filed as an exhibit to the Registration Statement, each such statement being qualified in all respects by such reference. A copy of the Registration Statement may be inspected without charge at the Commission's principal office in Washington, D.C., and copies of all or any part thereof may be obtained from the Commission upon the payment of certain fees prescribed by the Commission.

It would be fitting to close this chapter with a memorable story I read in the October 23, 1989 issue of *Forbes* about Robert VanKampen, bond fund guru and millionaire in his own right. I think you'll find it very revealing.

It seems that VanKampen made his millions in municipal bonds after cutting his teeth at the Chicago brokerage house of John Nuveen & Co. He quickly earned the name "Charger," and approached all of his accounts with zeal and professionalism. Six years of learning and selling led him to an income that out-earned that of Nuveen's chairman.

In 1967, at age 28, he started VanKampen Merritt and bought bonds wholesale from Nuveen and sold them at a slight markup to VanKampen's old customer base of small banks. By 1974, VanKampen was packaging bonds into tax-free funds as a result of customers' requests for AAA bonds. The funds were backed with insurance, which strengthened the rating and soon they were selling them through all of the major brokerage houses, allowing the houses to market them under their own names and making very nice commissions to boot.

It took VanKampen Merritt nine months to sell its first $5 million insured muni bond trusts. By 1983 the firm was selling $300 million a month of unit trusts. It is interesting to note that he sold his company to Xerox in late 1983. He was just 44 and made $185 million from the stock value of the sale.

The moral of the story is: Find a company that sells tax-exempt securities to the public and buy the stock of the company. VanKampen did.

Endnote

[1] Excerpted from page 135 of "How to Keep Your Savings Safe," by Walter L. Updegrave, Assoc. Ed, *Money* magazine.

6

Why Stocks Work: To Market, to Market, to Buy a Fat . . . Portfolio!

"Time is a liability when investing in bonds; however time is an asset when investing in stocks."
—Charles Fahy

I have a simple formula for those who want to get rich. It is based on two important rules: First, earn enough money to be able to save some. With that money, buy stocks. Second, don't sell or trade any stocks unless you are a real pro—and you probably aren't—so just leave them alone. Continue buying stocks and 20 years out, you will be rich.

Nice game plan, isn't it? If it's so simple, then why isn't everybody rich, you say?

Re-read the chapter on human nature and you'll find your answer. There are no magical, mystical ways of making money in the stock market. Actually, it can be quite boring most of the time. So if you are of the Las Vegas mentality and like to gamble with your money—speculate with options, commodities, and other risky products, this chapter is not for you. However, I do suggest you read it because it might show you the error of your ways if you are losing money with your own strategies.

You'll Make Money—Look at the Historical Proof!

The very first thing you must do before investing in any product is research it thoroughly. Check out all of the available data on the subject—historical and current. The historical data on the performance of the stock market is astounding and most of it is self-explanatory. I always show the well-known Ibbotson & Associates statistics (Figure 6.1), along with Table 6.1, the Long-Term View.

If you look at the historical side, the Ibbotson textbook proves that stocks are the number one money-making vehicle for the human race. I believe the proverbial complaint most people have about stocks is that you have to make sure you live long enough to realize any profits. In my opinion, that is rationalization.

The reality is that for every 10-year market cycle you have a 90 percent chance of making a profit. Over a 20-year cycle the odds are 100 percent. Just look at the Ibbotson chart

Figure 6-1   Wealth Indices of Investments in the U. S. Capital Markets (1926-1989) (Year-End 1925 = $1.00)

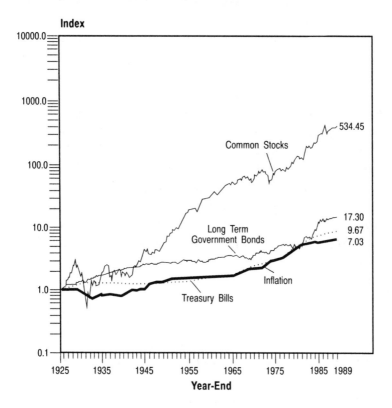

SOURCE: Ibbotson, Roger G., and Rex A. Sinquefield, *Stocks, Bonds, Bills, and Inflation* (SBBI), 1982 updated in *SBBI 1988 Yearbook,* Ibbotson Associates, Chicago.

for the 10-year period from 1978-1987 to see what happened to $1 invested in common stocks in 1979 as opposed to other investments. Stocks did $15.26 as opposed to long-term government bonds, which did $9.47. As a matter of fact, common stocks held over any 10-year period beat inflation 87 percent of the time since 1926. But long-term bonds held for 10 years failed to keep pace with inflation 60 percent of the time. A pretty good argument for stocks in favor of bonds, wouldn't you say?

Tilting the tables somewhat, there is a 24 percent chance you will lose some of your investment if you only hold your stocks for one year (See Table 6-1). As you continue to hold, though, your percentage goes down considerably. For example, if you hold your investments for five years, you have only a 6 percent chance of losing and a mere 1 percent chance over a 10-year period. Thus, if you are looking at guaranteeing your success rate for your retirement, you'll be happy to know that your chances for losing money in the stock market over a 20-year period drops to zero. (Note the market timing statistics in Table 6-1.) And that statistic proves why the company pension and retirement accounts always make money.

Table 6-1   The Long-Term View

Holding Period	Probability of Earning			Chance of Losing
	0-10%	10%-20%	over 20%	
1 Year	19%	19%	38%	24%
5 Years	30%	40%	24%	6%
10 Years	29%	54%	16%	1%
20 Years	22%	70%	8%	0%

SOURCE: Ibbotson Associates.

Don't Fight the System

The systematic approach to putting away money in a retirement fund is necessary to make your investments work. You need to put money away in good as well as bad markets. The classic investment approach used in the mutual fund industry that is extremely viable is called the "dollar cost averaging system." Simply put, this means investing a set amount at regular intervals. When prices dip, you'll be buying cheap shares. Dollar-cost averaging makes you save consistently, which is a major key to successful investing.

Remember the story about Joe, my wealthiest client in Chapter 3? Well, he was practicing dollar-cost averaging and he didn't even know it. Now, he has a retirement income of three times his last year's income!

Another true "buy and hold" story is a personal one, and one that I call my "mother-in-law portfolio strategy" story. When my father-in-law passed away, my mother-in-law and I decided to take a trip to the bank and go through their savings deposit box. She was extremely self-conscious and embarrassed, and said, "Gosh, Charlie, my husband and I really never did anything right with regards to investing. You are so smart about Wall Street, I know, but I want you to know that George was so sick for such a long time that all I had time to do was roll over the CDs and keep the stock certificates in the box."

Well, she kept apologizing all the way to the bank. And, when we got there and opened the box, I discovered—much to my surprise and delight—she had railroad and insurance company stock that was worth about $10,000 when they obtained it and now worth about $60,000. She had accumulated CDs right and left, so as it turned out, she was rich!

I chuckled and said, "Gosh, I wish I had clients across the board as smart as you." If an uneducated or inexperienced stockbroker or financial planner had gotten hold of her portfolio 10 years earlier, she would probably only have one-third of what she owns today.

Now, how many of you have socked away $100 per month for the last five years? I mean, just cash every month hidden underneath the mattress or in a lock box? That would be a hoard of 60 months x $100 or $6,000. If you did this for 10 years, you would have $12,000. If you saved $200 per month, the total would be $24,000. Have you followed this type of systematic savings?

Now, add the investment return factor. You've seen mutual funds ads that illustrate historical and hypothetical rates of return. What if you combined the growth rate of stocks to the monthly systematic savings plan (mattress method)? What rate of return could you expect? Let's take a look:

Mr. College Saver started a plan on December 1, 1981, by investing $1,500 in a high-flying mutual fund (See Table 6-2). Mr. Saver continued to invest $300 per month. By the end of 1982 he had invested $5,100 and his investment was worth $4,184, or a net loss of $915, down 17.9 percent. I can hear his complaints even now, "Stocks are nothing more than a gamble. I should have been in CDs." Not so fast. Mr. Saver may have bought some 5- or 10-year, high-yielding, fixed investment instruments. If he had been willing to invest for 5- and 10-year periods, let's look at what happened in the fifth and tenth year of this long-term stock growth program:

By 1986, he had invested $19,500 and the value of his investment was $30,602. A wonderful gain of $11,102, or +56 percent—an average annual gain of 11.2 percent. At this juncture, Mr. College Saver was a hero. Until the crash of 1987.

Figure 6-2 Dollar Cost Averaging Model

FIDELITY DESTINY I FUND

PREPARED FOR-------- AL FAHY

INITIAL INVESTMENT----------------------	$1,500.00
PLAN SIZE----------------------------------	$300.00
BREAKPOINT-------------------------------	$300.00
PAYMENT 1-12/13--- 50.00% ---------	$150.00
PAYMENT 12/13-300- 1.68% ---------	$5.04
CUSTODIAN FEE----------------------------	$1.50

START DATE-----------------------------	12/ 1/1981
END DATE--------------------------------	3/ 1/1992
BEGINNING SHARE BALANCE-------------	.000
CUMULATIVE INVESTMENT----------------	$38,400.00
ENDING SHARE BALANCE----------------	5,831.453
VALUE OF HOLDINGS--------------------	$96,102.34

DATE	NAV	DISTR. /SHARE	MAINT. FEE	MONTHLY INVEST.	DISTR. TO SHARES	INVEST. FOR SHARES	SHARES PURCH.	CUMUL. SHARES	CUMUL. INVEST.	VALUE OF HOLDINGS	PROFIT/ LOSS
								.000			
12/01/81	$9.22	$.00	$.00	$1,500.00	$.00	$745.00	80.803	80.803	$1,500.00	$745.00	$-755.00
01/01/82	$9.02	$.00	$.00	$300.00	$.00	$148.50	16.463	97.266	$1,800.00	$877.34	$-922.66
02/01/82	$8.82	$.00	$.00	$300.00	$.00	$148.50	16.837	114.103	$2,100.00	$1,006.39	$-1,093.61
03/01/82	$8.59	$.00	$.00	$300.00	$.00	$148.50	17.288	131.390	$2,400.00	$1,128.64	$-1,271.36
04/01/82	$8.70	$.00	$.00	$300.00	$.00	$148.50	17.069	148.459	$2,700.00	$1,291.60	$-1,408.40
05/01/82	$9.23	$.00	$.00	$300.00	$.00	$148.50	16.089	164.548	$3,000.00	$1,518.78	$-1,481.22
06/01/82	$8.91	$.00	$.00	$300.00	$.00	$148.50	16.667	181.215	$3,300.00	$1,614.62	$-1,685.38

(table continues)

Figure 6-2 Dollar Cost Averaging Model (continued)

DATE	NAV	DISTR. /SHARE	MAINT. FEE	MONTHLY INVEST.	DISTR. TO SHARES	INVEST. FOR SHARES	SHARES PURCH.	CUMUL. SHARES	CUMUL. INVEST.	VALUE OF HOLDINGS	PROFIT/ LOSS
07/01/82	$8.85	$.00	$.00	$300.00	$.00	$148.50	16.780	197.994	$3,600.00	$1,752.25	$-1,847.75
07/26/82	$8.17	$.68	$2.00	$.00	$132.64	$.00	16.235	214.229	$3,600.00	$1,750.25	$-1,849.75
08/01/82	$7.96	$.00	$.00	$300.00	$.00	$293.46	36.867	251.096	$3,900.00	$1,998.72	$-1,901.28
09/01/82	$8.76	$.00	$.00	$300.00	$.00	$293.46	33.500	284.596	$4,200.00	$2,493.06	$-1,706.94
10/01/82	$8.92	$.00	$.00	$300.00	$.00	$293.46	32.899	317.495	$4,500.00	$2,832.05	$-1,667.95
11/01/82	$10.33	$.00	$.00	$300.00	$.00	$293.46	28.409	345.903	$4,800.00	$3,573.18	$-1,226.82
12/01/82	$11.25	$.00	$.00	$300.00	$.00	$293.46	26.085	371.989	$5,100.00	$4,184.87	$-915.13
01/01/83	$11.43	$.00	$.00	$300.00	$.00	$293.46	25.675	397.663	$5,400.00	$4,545.29	$-854.71
02/02/83	$12.02	$.00	$.00	$300.00	$.00	$293.46	24.414	422.078	$5,700.00	$5,073.37	$-626.63
03/01/83	$12.75	$.00	$.00	$300.00	$.00	$293.46	23.016	445.094	$6,000.00	$5,674.95	$-325.05
04/01/83	$13.40	$.00	$.00	$300.00	$.00	$293.46	21.900	466.994	$6,300.00	$6,257.72	$-42.28
05/01/83	$14.66	$.00	$.00	$300.00	$.00	$293.46	20.018	487.012	$6,600.00	$7,139.59	$539.59
06/01/83	$15.09	$.00	$.00	$300.00	$.00	$293.46	19.447	506.459	$6,600.00	$7,642.47	$742.47
07/01/83	$15.88	$.00	$.00	$300.00	$.00	$293.46	18.480	524.939	$7,200.00	$8,336.03	$1,136.03
07/25/83	$13.43	$2.60	$2.00	$.00	$1,362.84	$.00	101.477	626.416	$7,200.00	$8,412.77	$1,212.77
08/01/83	$12.76	$.00	$.00	$300.00	$.00	$293.46	22.998	649.415	$7,500.00	$8,286.53	$786.53
09/01/83	$12.61	$.00	$.00	$300.00	$.00	$293.46	23.272	672.687	$7,800.00	$8,482.58	$682.58
10/01/83	$13.01	$.00	$.00	$300.00	$.00	$293.46	22.556	695.243	$8,100.00	$9,045.12	$945.12
11/01/83	$12.74	$.00	$.00	$300.00	$.00	$293.46	23.035	718.278	$8,100.00	$9,150.86	$750.86
12/01/83	$13.24	$.00	$.00	$300.00	$.00	$293.46	22.165	740.442	$8,700.00	$9,803.46	$1,103.46
01/01/84	$13.18	$.00	$.00	$300.00	$.00	$293.46	22.266	762.708	$9,000.00	$10,052.49	$1,052.49
02/01/84	$12.95	$.00	$.00	$300.00	$.00	$293.46	22.661	785.369	$9,300.00	$10,170.53	$870.53
03/01/84	$12.29	$.00	$.00	$300.00	$.00	$293.46	23.878	809.247	$9,600.00	$9,945.65	$345.65
04/01/84	$12.49	$.00	$.00	$300.00	$.00	$293.46	23.496	832.743	$9,900.00	$10,400.96	$500.96
05/01/84	$12.58	$.00	$.00	$300.00	$.00	$293.46	23.328	856.070	$10,200.00	$10,769.36	$569.36
06/01/84	$11.79	$.00	$.00	$300.00	$.00	$293.46	24.891	880.961	$10,500.00	$10,386.53	$-113.47
07/01/84	$12.12	$.00	$.00	$300.00	$.00	$293.46	24.213	905.174	$10,800.00	$10,970.70	$170.70
07/30/84	$9.88	$2.05	$2.00	$.00	$1,853.61	$.00	187.612	1,092.785	$10,800.00	$10,796.72	$-3.28
08/01/84	$9.93	$.00	$.00	$300.00	$.00	$293.46	29.553	1,122.338	$11,100.00	$11,144.82	$44.82
09/01/84	$11.14	$.00	$.00	$300.00	$.00	$293.46	26.343	1,148.681	$11,400.00	$12,796.31	$1,396.31

Figure 6-2　Dollar Cost Averaging Model (continued)

DATE	NAV	DISTR. /SHARE	MAINT. FEE	MONTHLY INVEST.	DISTR. TO SHARES	INVEST. FOR SHARES	SHARES PURCH.	CUMUL. SHARES	CUMUL. INVEST.	VALUE OF HOLDINGS	PROFIT/ LOSS
10/01/84	$11.02	$.00	$.00	$300.00	$.00	$293.46	26.630	1,175.311	$11,700.00	$12,951.93	$1,251.93
11/01/84	$11.13	$.00	$.00	$300.00	$.00	$293.46	26.367	1,201.678	$12,000.00	$13,374.67	$1,374.67
12/01/84	$11.11	$.00	$.00	$300.00	$.00	$293.46	26.414	1,228.092	$12,300.00	$13,644.10	$1,344.10
01/01/85	$11.44	$.00	$.00	$300.00	$.00	$293.46	25.652	1,253.744	$12,600.00	$14,342.83	$1,742.83
02/01/85	$12.43	$.00	$.00	$300.00	$.00	$293.46	23.609	1,277.353	$12,900.00	$15,877.49	$2,977.49
03/01/85	$12.27	$.00	$.00	$300.00	$.00	$293.46	23.917	1,301.270	$13,200.00	$15,966.58	$2,766.58
04/01/85	$12.15	$.00	$.00	$300.00	$.00	$293.46	24.153	1,325.423	$13,500.00	$16,103.89	$2,603.89
05/01/85	$11.97	$.00	$.00	$300.00	$.00	$293.46	24.516	1,349.939	$13,800.00	$16,158.77	$2,358.77
06/01/85	$12.56	$.00	$.00	$300.00	$.00	$293.46	23.365	1,373.304	$14,100.00	$17,248.69	$3,148.69
07/01/85	$12.81	$.00	$.00	$300.00	$.00	$293.46	22.909	1,396.212	$14,400.00	$17,885.48	$3,485.48
08/01/85	$12.98	$.00	$.00	$300.00	$.00	$293.46	22.609	1,418.821	$14,700.00	$18,416.30	$3,716.30
08/12/85	$11.21	$1.60	$5.52	$.00	$2,264.59	$.00	202.015	1,620.836	$14,700.00	$18,169.58	$3,469.58
09/01/85	$11.21	$.00	$.00	$300.00	$.00	$293.46	26.178	1,647.015	$15,000.00	$18,463.05	$3,463.05
10/01/85	$10.80	$.00	$.00	$300.00	$.00	$293.46	27.172	1,674.187	$15,300.00	$18,081.22	$2,781.22
11/01/85	$11.33	$.00	$.00	$300.00	$.00	$293.46	25.901	1,700.088	$15,600.00	$19,262.00	$3,662.00
12/01/85	$12.26	$.00	$.00	$300.00	$.00	$293.46	23.936	1,724.025	$15,900.00	$21,136.54	$5,236.54
01/01/86	$12.92	$.00	$.00	$300.00	$.00	$293.46	22.714	1,746.738	$16,200.00	$22,567.86	$6,367.86
02/01/86	$13.24	$.00	$.00	$300.00	$.00	$293.46	22.165	1,768.903	$16,500.00	$23,420.27	$6,920.27
03/01/86	$14.57	$.00	$.00	$300.00	$.00	$293.46	20.141	1,789.044	$16,800.00	$26,056.37	$9,266.37
04/01/86	$15.53	$.00	$.00	$300.00	$.00	$293.46	18.896	1,807.941	$17,100.00	$28,077.32	$10,977.32
05/01/86	$15.48	$.00	$.00	$300.00	$.00	$293.46	18.957	1,826.898	$17,400.00	$28,280.38	$10,880.38
06/01/86	$15.94	$.00	$.00	$300.00	$.00	$293.46	18.410	1,845.308	$17,700.00	$29,414.21	$11,714.21
07/01/86	$16.04	$.00	$.00	$300.00	$.00	$293.46	18.296	1,863.604	$18,000.00	$29,892.20	$11,892.20
08/01/86	$14.87	$.00	$.00	$300.00	$.00	$293.46	19.735	1,883.339	$18,300.00	$28,005.25	$9,705.25
08/11/86	$12.29	$2.86	$5.06	$.00	$5,381.29	$.00	437.859	2,321.198	$18,300.00	$28,527.52	$10,227.52

(table continues)

Figure 6-2 Dollar Cost Averaging Model (continued)

DATE	NAV	DISTR. /SHARE	MAINT. FEE	MONTHLY INVEST.	DISTR. TO SHARES	INVEST. FOR SHARES	SHARES PURCH.	CUMUL. SHARES	CUMUL. INVEST.	VALUE OF HOLDINGS	PROFIT/ LOSS
09/01/86	$12.89	$.00	$.00	$300.00	$.00	$293.46	22.766	2,343.964	$18,600.00	$30,213.70	$11,613.70
10/01/86	$11.89	$.00	$.00	$300.00	$.00	$293.46	24.681	2,368.646	$18,900.00	$28,163.20	$9,263.20
11/01/86	$12.47	$.00	$.00	$300.00	$.00	$293.46	23.533	2,392.179	$19,200.00	$29,830.47	$10,630.47
12/01/86	$12.67	$.00	$.00	$300.00	$.00	$293.46	23.162	2,415.341	$19,500.00	$30,602.37	$11,102.37
01/01/87	$12.43	$.00	$.00	$300.00	$.00	$293.46	23.609	2,438.950	$19,800.00	$30,316.14	$10,516.14
02/01/87	$14.08	$.00	$.00	$300.00	$.00	$293.46	20.842	2,459.792	$20,100.00	$34,633.87	$14,533.87
03/01/87	$15.02	$.00	$.00	$300.00	$.00	$293.46	19.538	2,479.330	$20,400.00	$37,239.54	$16,839.54
04/01/87	$15.19	$.00	$.00	$300.00	$.00	$293.46	19.319	2,498.649	$20,700.00	$37,954.48	$17,254.48
05/01/87	$15.18	$.00	$.00	$300.00	$.00	$293.46	19.332	2,517.981	$21,000.00	$38,222.96	$17,222.96
06/01/87	$15.29	$.00	$.00	$300.00	$.00	$293.46	19.193	2,537.174	$21,300.00	$38,793.39	$17,493.39
07/01/87	$15.93	$.00	$.00	$300.00	$.00	$293.46	18.422	2,555.596	$21,600.00	$40,710.65	$19,110.65
08/01/87	$16.89	$.00	$.00	$300.00	$.00	$293.46	17.375	2,572.971	$21,900.00	$43,457.48	$21,557.48
08/31/87	$15.23	$2.58	$5.25	$.00	$6,633.01	$.00	435.523	3,008.494	$21,900.00	$45,819.36	$23,919.36
09/01/87	$15.21	$.00	$.00	$300.00	$.00	$293.46	19.294	3,027.788	$22,200.00	$46,052.65	$23,852.65
10/01/87	$14.85	$.00	$.00	$300.00	$.00	$293.46	19.762	3,047.549	$22,500.00	$45,256.11	$22,756.11
11/01/87	$11.08	$.00	$.00	$300.00	$.00	$293.46	26.486	3,074.035	$22,800.00	$34,060.31	$11,260.31
12/01/87	$10.13	$.00	$.00	$300.00	$.00	$293.46	28.969	3,103.004	$23,100.00	$31,433.43	$8,333.43
12/17/87	$10.10	$.80	$.00	$.00	$2,482.40	$.00	245.783	3,348.787	$23,100.00	$33,822.75	$10,722.75
01/01/88	$10.43	$.00	$.00	$300.00	$.00	$293.46	28.136	3,376.923	$23,400.00	$35,221.31	$11,821.31
02/01/88	$10.81	$.00	$.00	$300.00	$.00	$293.46	27.147	3,404.070	$23,700.00	$36,798.00	$13,098.00
03/01/88	$11.57	$.00	$.00	$300.00	$.00	$293.46	25.364	3,429.434	$24,000.00	$39,678.55	$15,678.55
04/01/88	$11.30	$.00	$.00	$300.00	$.00	$293.46	25.970	3,455.404	$24,300.00	$39,046.06	$14,746.06

Figure 6-2   Dollar Cost Averaging Model (continued)

DATE	NAV	DISTR. /SHARE	MAINT. FEE	MONTHLY INVEST.	DISTR. TO SHARES	INVEST. FOR SHARES	SHARES PURCH.	CUMUL. SHARES	CUMUL. INVEST.	VALUE OF HOLDINGS	PROFIT/ LOSS
05/01/88	$11.55	$.00	$.00	$300.00	$.00	$293.46	25.408	3,480.812	$24,600.00	$40,203.37	$15,603.37
06/01/88	$11.60	$.00	$.00	$300.00	$.00	$293.46	25.298	3,506.110	$24,900.00	$40,670.87	$15,770.87
07/01/88	$12.44	$.00	$.00	$300.00	$.00	$293.46	23.590	3,529.700	$25,200.00	$43,909.47	$18,709.47
08/01/88	$12.32	$.00	$.00	$300.00	$.00	$293.46	23.820	3,553.520	$25,500.00	$43,779.36	$18,279.36
08/26/88	$11.38	$.32	$5.46	$.00	$1,131.67	$.00	99.443	3,652.963	$25,500.00	$41,570.72	$16,070.72
09/01/88	$11.47	$.00	$.00	$300.00	$.00	$293.46	25.585	3,678.548	$25,800.00	$42,192.95	$16,392.95
10/01/88	$11.92	$.00	$.00	$300.00	$.00	$293.46	24.619	3,703.167	$26,100.00	$44,141.75	$18,041.75
11/01/88	$12.08	$.00	$.00	$300.00	$.00	$293.46	24.293	3,727.460	$26,400.00	$44,027.72	$18,627.72
12/01/88	$11.80	$.00	$.00	$300.00	$.00	$293.46	24.869	3,752.330	$26,700.00	$44,277.49	$17,577.49
12/19/88	$11.89	$.20	$.00	$.00	$750.47	$.00	63.117	3,815.447	$26,700.00	$45,365.67	$18,665.67
01/01/89	$11.91	$.00	$.00	$300.00	$.00	$293.46	24.640	3,840.087	$27,000.00	$45,735.44	$18,735.44
02/01/89	$12.93	$.00	$.00	$300.00	$.00	$293.46	22.696	3,862.783	$27,300.00	$49,945.79	$22,645.79
03/01/89	$12.64	$.00	$.00	$300.00	$.00	$293.46	23.217	3,886.000	$27,600.00	$49,119.04	$21,519.04
04/01/89	$12.93	$.00	$.00	$300.00	$.00	$293.46	22.696	3,908.696	$27,900.00	$50,539.44	$22,639.44
05/01/89	$13.52	$.00	$.00	$300.00	$.00	$293.46	21.706	3,930.402	$28,200.00	$53,139.03	$24,939.03
06/01/89	$14.35	$.00	$.00	$300.00	$.00	$293.46	20.450	3,950.852	$28,500.00	$56,694.72	$28,194.72
07/01/89	$14.03	$.00	$.00	$300.00	$.00	$293.46	20.917	3,971.768	$28,800.00	$55,723.91	$26,923.91
08/01/89	$14.97	$.00	$.00	$300.00	$.00	$293.46	19.603	3,991.372	$29,100.00	$59,750.83	$30,650.83
08/22/89	$14.61	$.64	$5.74	$.00	$2,548.74	$.00	174.452	4,165.823	$29,100.00	$60,862.68	$31,762.68
09/01/89	$14.73	$.00	$.00	$300.00	$.00	$293.46	19.923	4,185.746	$29,400.00	$61,656.03	$32,256.03
10/01/89	$14.85	$.00	$.00	$300.00	$.00	$293.46	19.762	4,205.507	$29,700.00	$62,461.78	$32,751.78
11/01/89	$14.35	$.00	$.00	$300.00	$.00	$293.46	20.450	4,225.958	$30,000.00	$60,642.49	$30,642.49
12/01/89	$14.42	$.00	$.00	$300.00	$.00	$293.46	20.351	4,246.308	$30,300.00	$61,231.77	$30,931.77
12/11/89	$13.43	$.79	$.00	$.00	$3,354.58	$.00	249.783	4,496.091	$30,300.00	$60,382.51	$30,082.51
01/01/90	$13.54	$.00	$.00	$300.00	$.00	$293.46	21.674	4,517.765	$30,600.00	$61,170.54	$30,570.54

(table continues)

Figure 6-2   Dollar Cost Averaging Model (continued)

DATE	NAV	DISTR. /SHARE	MAINT. FEE	MONTHLY INVEST.	DISTR. TO SHARES	INVEST. FOR SHARES	SHARES PURCH.	CUMUL. SHARES	CUMUL. INVEST.	VALUE OF HOLDINGS	PROFIT/ LOSS
02/01/90	$12.73	$.00	$.00	$300.00	$.00	$293.46	23.053	4,540.817	$30,900.00	$57,804.61	$26,904.61
03/01/90	$13.00	$.00	$.00	$300.00	$.00	$293.46	22.574	4,563.391	$31,200.00	$59,324.09	$28,124.09
04/01/90	$13.28	$.00	$.00	$300.00	$.00	$293.46	22.098	4,585.489	$31,500.00	$60,895.30	$29,395.30
05/01/90	$12.85	$.00	$.00	$300.00	$.00	$293.46	22.837	4,608.327	$31,800.00	$59,217.00	$27,417.00
06/01/90	$14.27	$.00	$.00	$300.00	$.00	$293.46	20.565	4,628.891	$32,100.00	$66,054.28	$33,954.28
07/01/90	$14.24	$.00	$.00	$300.00	$.00	$293.46	20.608	4,649.500	$32,400.00	$66,208.87	$33,808.87
08/01/90	$13.84	$.00	$.00	$300.00	$.00	$293.46	21.204	4,670.703	$32,700.00	$64,642.53	$31,942.53
08/03/90	$12.67	$.59	$6.01	$.00	$2,749.70	$.00	217.025	4,887.728	$32,700.00	$61,927.52	$29,227.52
09/01/90	$11.87	$.00	$.00	$300.00	$.00	$293.46	24.723	4,912.451	$33,000.00	$58,310.79	$25,310.79
10/01/90	$11.07	$.00	$.00	$300.00	$.00	$293.46	26.509	4,938.960	$33,300.00	$54,674.29	$21,374.29
11/01/90	$10.99	$.00	$.00	$300.00	$.00	$293.46	26.702	4,965.663	$33,600.00	$54,572.64	$20,972.64
12/01/90	$11.93	$.00	$.00	$300.00	$.00	$293.46	24.598	4,990.261	$33,900.00	$59,533.82	$25,633.82
01/01/91	$12.53	$.00	$.00	$300.00	$.00	$293.46	23.421	5,013.682	$34,200.00	$62,821.44	$28,621.44
02/01/91	$13.88	$.00	$.00	$300.00	$.00	$293.46	21.143	5,034.825	$34,500.00	$69,883.37	$35,383.37
03/01/91	$14.84	$.00	$.00	$300.00	$.00	$293.46	19.775	5,054.600	$34,800.00	$75,010.26	$40,210.26
04/01/91	$15.19	$.00	$.00	$300.00	$.00	$293.46	19.319	5,073.919	$35,100.00	$77,072.83	$41,972.83
05/01/91	$15.38	$.00	$.00	$300.00	$.00	$293.46	19.081	5,092.999	$35,400.00	$78,330.33	$42,930.33
06/01/91	$16.30	$.00	$.00	$300.00	$.00	$293.46	18.004	5,111.003	$35,700.00	$83,309.35	$47,609.35

Figure 6-2 Dollar Cost Averaging Model (continued)

DATE	NAV	DISTR. /SHARE	MAINT. FEE	MONTHLY INVEST.	DISTR. TO SHARES	INVEST. FOR SHARES	SHARES PURCH.	CUMUL. SHARES	CUMUL. INVEST.	VALUE OF HOLDINGS	PROFIT/ LOSS
07/01/91	$15.23	$.00	$.00	$300.00	$.00	$293.46	19.269	5,130.272	$36,000.00	$78,134.04	$42,134.04
08/01/91	$16.24	$.00	$.00	$300.00	$.00	$293.46	18.070	5,148.342	$36,300.00	$83,609.07	$47,309.07
08/09/91	$15.58	$.76	$6.29	$.00	$3,906.45	$.00	250.735	5,399.077	$36,300.00	$84,117.62	$47,817.62
09/01/91	$16.01	$.00	$.00	$300.00	$.00	$293.46	18.330	5,417.407	$36,600.00	$86,732.68	$50,132.68
10/01/91	$15.74	$.00	$.00	$300.00	$.00	$293.46	18.644	5,436.051	$36,900.00	$85,563.44	$48,663.44
11/01/91	$15.67	$.00	$.00	$300.00	$.00	$293.46	18.728	5,454.778	$37,200.00	$85,476.38	$48,276.38
12/01/91	$14.71	$.00	$.00	$300.00	$.00	$293.46	19.950	5,474.728	$37,500.00	$80,533.25	$43,033.25
12/13/91	$14.33	$.79	$.00	$.00	$4,325.04	$.00	301.817	5,776.545	$37,500.00	$82,777.89	$45,277.89
01/01/92	$15.74	$.00	$.00	$300.00	$.00	$293.46	18.644	5,795.189	$37,800.00	$91,216.28	$53,416.28
02/01/92	$15.90	$.00	$.00	$300.00	$.00	$293.46	18.457	5,813.646	$38,100.00	$92,436.97	$54,336.97
03/01/92	$16.48	$.00	$.00	$300.00	$.00	$293.46	17.807	5,831.453	$38,400.00	$96,102.34	$57,702.34

In August of 1987, his account was riding a $23,919 profit on $21,900 invested. This was a 109 percent profit in five and a half years, or an annual average of 19.8 percent. Then came the crash of 1987 leaving a December '87 balance of $34,060 on his $22,800 investment. His profit was now only $8,333, or 36 percent for six years—or an average of 6 percent per year. Can you hear the complaining? "I should have been conservative with this college money and bought those high-yield, fixed investments or even CDs."

Again, not so fast. He actually continued the plan knowing he had the opportunity to buy more shares at lower prices with his $300 monthly contribution and the dividend reinvestment plan.

By September 1991, he now had a $50,132 profit on his investment of $36,600. This was a 135 percent gain in almost nine years, or a 15 percent increase per year. The recent "recession market" of late 1991 lowered his profit to $43,000 in November of 1991. It seemed we had nothing but bad news and his son was in his senior year.

A few months later, his account recovered. On March 1, 1992, his account was valued at $96,102! His son was accepted into the University of Tennessee. Mr. College Saver has invested $38,400 to date and had a $57,702 gain. The university's estimated annual budget per student is approximately $5,000 per year. Mr. Saver can afford to send his son to UT with plenty to spare. Good thing, too, because he now has two daughters right behind the son, in their junior and sophomore years in high school.

This was one client I certainly wanted to be successful. Mr. College Saver is my older and *bigger* brother!

In case you need further proof, just ask anyone 65 or older who is living on Social Security if they wish they would have socked away a little money each month for stocks. Ask people who lived through the crash what their financial situation would be today had they bought stocks in 1929 and 1933. They would have bought in at approximately 380 and the Dow is over 3000 today. Look at that capital appreciation!

A Clearer Definition of "Buy Low, Sell High"

Now, if you are a more experienced investor and feel you must trade the market, let me say this. You must learn to buy into the market when it's depressed as it was in July of 1974, August of 1982, or during the crash of October, 1987. When you invest in what you feel is a "buy" market, but are too early—don't lose your cool. Be assured it will recover and go to new highs. If you buy quality stocks, they will follow the market. On the other hand, if you are a new or fairly inexperienced investor, you should stick with stock funds in the early stages of your investing program. These stock funds provide immediate diversification (which we'll discuss later in the chapter) and professional management as well. Jonathan Pond, editor of Wiesenberger Mutual Funds Investment Report suggests that after a portfolio exceeds $20,000, you can begin to make decisions about individual stocks and stock industries. He also agrees that maintaining a permanent portfolio structure, or system, forces you to buy low and sell high. To quote Mr. Pond, "Don't be surprised if you find yourself selling stocks when the pundits say there's no limit on how far stocks will continue to rise, and buying stocks when the experts proclaim the Great Bear Market. This is exactly what you should be doing and you will benefit over the long run."

James W. Michaels, editor of *Forbes* magazine, says in his June 24, 1991 letter, "The time to buy securities is when the media are so full of doom that your trembling hand can scarcely hold the telephone to call your broker with a buy order The time to sell is when those same people say that stocks can 'only go up.'" Enough said.

Dow Hits 10,000: The Super Cyclical Cycle

I am a firm believer that the Dow Jones Industrial Average will hit the 10,000 mark by the year 2000. Do you think that's far-fetched? Let's take a look again at history and let me explain what I call the "Super Cyclical Cycle" of the stock market.

If you examine the most popular of the market indices, the Dow, you'll learn that it traded in the 40-point level as we came into the 1900s. By 1929, it hit 384, almost ten times higher in 29 years. This is the first "Super Cyclical Cycle" of the century. These super cycles, in simple terms, have two phases. Phase One is an extended period of time when the market trades sideways for a while, say 12 to 15 years. The 40 to 60 point level traded from 1900 to 1917. 1917 was a turning point where the market started an uptrend taking the Dow from the 40 level to the 384 level by 1929. Now, this would be the beginning of the second phase of the cycle. This uptrend is volatile, taking two or three steps up, one back or four steps up, one back and so on. In other words, within this expanding market, there can be many down-turns.

In the 1930s, the second Super Cyclical Cycle had a Phase One trend going sideways around the 100 level on the Dow. This 100-200 range lasted from 1935-1943. By that time, the second phase took the market up to 1000 by 1966. In other words, from the 100s in the 1930s to 1000 in the 1960s, there was a tenfold move for the second time in this century.

Now, for the third time, the market based a pattern of trading in the 1000 Dow level for 16 years, or until 1982 when it turned up with volatility—yet more up than down—and carried it to the 3000 mark in 1991. It made a big step back in October of 1987 during the crash (in just one day!), yet it is back to those levels as usual. More than likely, if history continues on its course, this expansion of Phase Two of the Super Cyclical Cycle will continue until it reaches the 10,000 zone. A simple calculation will prove that your money will triple in 10 years if history proves my theory true. Now let me give you a few more specific examples of historical events and how they affected the stock market.

History Makes Money; Money Makes History

I read with interest an ad that a large regional brokerage firm ran in the *Wall Street Journal* a few years back. The ad documented what $10,000 invested at times of various historical calamities would be worth today. For example, in 1962, the missile crisis brought us close to World War III. At that time, if you had invested $10,000, the value today would be $156,661. In 1965, we bombed North Vietnam and were attacked in the Gulf of Tonkin. The value of $10,000 invested then would now be worth $109,602. In 1968, there was a six-day war in the Middle East and five days of rioting in Detroit; the value of $10,000 invested then would now be worth $87,429. In 1980, Iran was holding American hostages; the value of $10,000 invested then would now be worth $48,700. The recession in 1982 caused the market to hit 730 in August and by February the following year the market was up 57 percent to 1150. On October, 1987, the country saw the most severe drop in market history. $10,000 invested at the bottom of the market on October 20 would be worth approximately $24,000 today.

(As an aside, a great story from that crash concerns John Templeton, the most respected value investor of our time, and his "submarine orders." As the story goes, Templeton was reported to have said that he didn't know where the bottom of the market would settle. Being the astute investor that he was, he had his traders enter orders well below the last known price. They were referred to as his "submarine orders." For example, in the hectic trading of that day, the last reported trade of a stock could have been at 50 when the day before it might have been at 60. Not knowing if it was still trading at 50 or not, he would send in his orders to buy at 42 and in the panic—if he got lucky—his trade would get executed at 42. His orders were dubbed submarine orders because no one knew where the bottom was. He used his knowledge of the market and his investing instinct.)

Three years later, the 1990 Gulf War drove the market down from the 2750 mark to a 2300 low. And in the midst of the war, the economic burdens were being touted in the media as deeply affecting the budget and warning of a second dip recession. What was amazing was how the market shot up in just a few weeks after the war from 2450 to 2800! These down markets caused by crisis events are opportunities only if you have cash available to seize the opportunity of the moment of the down markets. If you are caught fully invested in stocks when these events occur and your stocks go down, ride them out and stay fully invested as the market always recovers and, given time, eventually heads to new record highs. (See Figure 3-1.)

As an investor, when historical events have you scared, "keep in mind that bailing out of stocks, with the idea of jumping back in later, is how most individual investors get burned," wrote Jim Henderson in *USA Today* on August 23, 1990, in an article entitled, "Surviving a Long-Term Slump."

Now back to our statistics. From 1982 to 1987, the bull market ran from 730 to 2850. This includes 1,276 trading days. If you had been invested for 1,276 days, your annual return would have been 26.3 percent. If you were out of the market for 40 of the best days—or 3 percent of the days—your annual return would have dropped to 4.3 percent!! In other words, if by trying to time the market, you missed 3 percent of the best days that usually follow the worst days, you forfeit 84 percent of your potential recovery. It doesn't pay to panic and give up. It's like jumping off the ship in a storm into stormier waters. Stay on board. When you get to land, you will appreciate having had the courage to stay on board even though you were frightened during the storm.

Petrochemical Plants and Stocks Don't Work

Here's another analogy. I often drive to the ARCO Petrochemical complex in Pasadena, Texas, to lecture their employees on investing. One day, I drove to the refinery. Once there, I had to drive slowly and cautiously past the many "Danger" signs posted every few feet. Finally, I arrived at the lecture hall in a cold sweat. My knowledge of refineries was limited to what I hear from the news media—facilities blow up, people are killed, cancer develops; in general everything appears to look dangerous. Let a valve hiss or go off and I come close to having a heart attack. Yet, when I looked around the room at the employees, they were happily chatting away with their colleagues. They weren't worried! Why not? Because they understood the refinery operations and coming to the refinery was part of their daily work routine. Yet I stood there, about to give a speech, in a cold sweat!

It's the same feeling for the refinery employee, teacher, pilot, doctor etc. who walks into the world of investing. As a professional investment advisor I know that, traditionally, the market always goes back up—maybe not at the rate and consistency we like, but it does go back up. The $64,000 question is, will you be in the market when it does?

World Economic Changes

You are probably wondering at this point what underlying economics propelled the stock market in the past to such levels and what will happen to ensure market upturns. Well, we've all had basic economic courses which point out that the war economy bodes well for corporate values. The most fundamental analogy can be made with a struggling, young company making a consumer product like a tractor. A tractor bought by a farmer is built to last and is probably well taken care of by that farmer. Yet, the same company, during the war, might be asked to make tanks. The tank is meant for battle and certainly won't last as long as the farmer's tractor. Therefore, the company will produce more tanks than tractors.

As the country gears up for the manufacture of war products, productivity goes up. Increased productivity is usually the result of bad news. Simply put, it means the same number of employees will build more products or half the employees will build the same number. When war breaks out, it usually causes an immediate stock market sell-off in a big way. Then the pattern proves that within 90 days or so the market recovers from the sell-off and climbs for almost 24 months, ascending 50 percent to 100 percent higher.

For example, in late 1953, the Korean War sent the market down 15 percent initially and then up over 100 percent by 1956.

And, if you examine the benchmark years, you will discover common economic occurrences. In 1917, world change as a result of the impact of World War I. In the 1940s, again a transition in the world with the Second World War. In 1982, what we will probably look back on and see as the beginning of world change due to U.S. capitalism. We saw the crash of 1987 and the 1990 war in the Persian Gulf.

Now there are major currents of positive world economic changes that will fire up not only our economy, but also the superpowers as military defense monies shift to consumer manufacturing monies. Here is where the monies will flow to propel the stock market to the 10,000 level.

Pension funds have more cash available than the value of all stocks in the U.S. today. In addition, IRA and personal pension dollars projected to be deposited in the next 10 years are also greater than the entire value of U.S. stock today. Look at the once-again healthy Social Security fund which is required to reinvest its surpluses in the U.S. Treasury agency instruments. This helps reduce interest rates and this, in turn, reduces the U.S. budget deficit. Continue the scenario by factoring in the baby boomers who are entering their savings years. You can add the foreign investors who will continue to invest in the U.S. These positive trends are in force and are working in our favor in this era. We are working towards a 10,000 Dow. Much of this will be written about as it all unfolds in the 1990s. Over time, history has shown we will survive and do better in all areas of commerce and trade. You should be fully invested in stocks as this occurs. Don't sit back and watch others take advantage of the trends—seize the opportunities as they present themselves. Remember eras of increased productivity and up-market cycles are full of bad news as change causes skepticism.

Which Stocks to Pick?

Ah, now that is the trick. Let me tell you a little story about stock picking that taught me a big lesson back in the mid-1970s. I did research on a company called Jetero that had invested $20 million in apartment complexes back in 1956. Well, it didn't take a rocket scientist to figure out that because of rapid inflation, the oil boom, and the increase in housing activity, this property was worth considerably more than when it was purchased 20 years ago. The stock was trading at $6 per share and the way I figured it, the apartments were worth at least $40 million, if not $60 million, on the market. The company was solid.

Well, I put 20 clients in the stock and six months later we were in a bear market and the stock dropped all the way to $2. I lost half of my 20 clients, leaving 10 clients remaining. Over the next six months, the stock worked itself back up to $6 and another half of my remaining 10 clients were happy to get out, leaving five clients. In essence, the stock had gone from $6 to $6 in 12 months. Two more months passed and the stock moved up to $8 per share. At that time, three more of my clients took their profits and got out, leaving two clients. So, 18 out of 20 clients either lost money, broke even or made nothing more then they would have if they had invested in a CD. Then two months later, the stock jumped to $14 and the remaining two clients were happy because they had doubled their money. That's not a very good track record, though. And that one of the two clients was my son—he couldn't fire me—meant only one client made money on a company I had thoroughly researched and believed in.

That was so frustrating for me. But that's when I learned the cardinal rules of investing: Don't give in to human nature, invest for the long term, have a system, and diversify.

Diversify, Diversify, Diversify

Now diversification is an absolute necessity—something I didn't fully realize when I put my 20 clients in Jetero. You can create a large degree of tolerance in your stock portfolio when you diversify. For example, if you have one stock that goes down, obviously your entire system performs poorly. So, if you study the conventional wisdom of diversification by such investors as Warren Buffet or John Templeton, you'll find you should use a 5 percent allocation system.

Simply put, don't put more than 5 percent in any one stock idea. The reason being if one of your stocks go to zero, all you can lose is 5 percent with a 5 percent allocation system. One out of ten stocks might go to zero, but one out of ten will double or triple. One stock out of 20 might go ten-fold. So, the superwinners will more than compensate for your losses. Buying only one stock issue or investing in only one industry assumes that your choice will outperform all others. That action in and of itself is risky and the average individual investor should not take any unnecessary risks. Table 6-3 on diversification will clearly show the advantages of this type of system.

Diversification should always be coupled with discipline. Discipline is derived from a technique of identifying individual securities in your diversified portfolio. If you don't have experience and knowledge, then you need to stay

Table 6-3   Diversification Chart

Number of Issues in Portfolio	Percent of Total Risk	Percent by Which Risk Reduced	Cumulative Risk Reduction
1	100%	0%	0%
2	80	20	20
3	75	5	25
4	70	5	30
5	65	5	35
6	60	5	40
7	58	2	42
8	56	2	44
9	54	2	46
10	52	2	48
15	47	5	53
20	45	2	55

SOURCE: Peter D. Heerwagen, *Investing for Total Return* (Chicago: Probus, 1988). p. 32.

with the diversification system and ride it through. Another reason to diversify is that none of us can predit the future of various economies and industries. We can calculate, surmise, and forcast but, I submit, none of us can pinpoint both the exact time and place that events will occur affecting stocks in those various industries. To illustrate, let me tell you about the "Rainbow Effect."

Not a year goes by that there is not a highly-visible, well-known doomsayer charting trends and forecasting the economy and the market in highly academic terms. I started noticing this in 1972 with the "gold bugs" speaking of economic malaise and advising us to buy gold at $800 an ounce. Gold hit $1,000 an ounce and they were right on target. Then, of course, we have had a "correction" in price since then for almost 15 years.

I attribute this constant shift of the limelight on these temporary experts to the "Rainbow Effect." In other words, we can all agree that the rainbow exists, but we cannot agree on where it will appear next. If the rainbow appears over a particular economic sector, that particular sector economist is the new expert! When the rainbow covered the oil and gas industry, for example, as it did in late 1989, that group of stocks became the new hot stocks. The rainbow goes on its way, randomly popping here and there. If we only knew where it would appear in the future, we could find that pot of gold. Yet, it cannot be predicted.

So, am I sticking my neck out and saying that experts cannot predict with consistency? Yes, I am saying exactly that. If you learn nothing but this one lesson from the book, you will be far ahead of the investment game.

Today, there are numerous experts expressing their future trends. At any given time, almost all possibilities are covered by predictions. Again, and after the fact, we'll hear who was the most accurate and that person will be the expert of the moment. Remember the adage, "A stopped clock is correct twice a day."

So what have you learned from all of this? Don't—I repeat, don't—look at forecasting to help your investing program. Look for proven performance over a significant time frame. I can't stress this enough. The longer your data base of results, the better for your stock portfolio.

Remember, instead of forecasting or predicting, simply diversify. And while diversification prevents portfolio catastrophe, it does not necessarily present opportunity. Only time can do that.

Blood Pressure vs. Interest Rates and How They Relate to Stocks

We've all come to understand that if interest rates fall, that's good for the stock market and if they go up, it's bad. Then, there's the correlation in people's minds that if bonds go up in value, that's good for the stock market because interest rates are going down. However, in the last decade, for example, this concept hasn't held true and it has confused a lot of people. This was true from the 1930s until the 1960s, but then something happened in the 1970s that changed things. And let me explain it with an analogy:

Let's say interest rates are like our blood pressure. Interest rates monitor the flow—it's a pressure gauge of the flow of money through the economy. Think of money as blood circulating through your veins. If interest rates get high—blood pressure gets high—it may be because you are jogging. If the interest rates go higher (your blood pressure gets higher), it is probably because you are now sprinting. But, everything is still fine. Now, you're really moving out. The economy is moving and everything is wonderful. The economy and the human body are on a great sprint. But, if you have a situation where the interest rates go even higher (your blood pressure goes even higher) and into a danger zone—that's bad news. Because now what's happening is you're not sprinting anymore, you are racing for your life. You are on the verge of a heart attack. Something is wrong and your body is clamping down, it's trying to tell you something. Now, interest rates are way too high and there is a credit squeeze. Your body—and the economy—is fighting for its life.

You see, rising interest rates are not necessarily a sign of bad news for the stock market. The 1980s proved that. We

Dr. Ravi Batra, PhD., author of The Crash of 1990 *on "Money Talks" with host–author Charles Fahy: Dr. Batra wrote a sensational book that hit the nation's best seller list. Some refer to this book as famous, others infamous. When Dr. Batra appeared on the show in April of 1990, the Dow Jones Index was at the 2700 level. Since then, it has risen to over 3400. So far, there has been no crash in 1990 through 1993.*

had a rapid rise in rates from 1982 until 1986 and the stock market went through the roof. The Dow went from 1000 to 2000 in that period of time. It was simply an indication of a vivacious sprint in our economy.

Now, when interest rates fall to, say, below 4 percent , there's no demand for money. So, no one wants money and what we begin to see is an economy coming to a standstill as it did in 1992. This is also true of your blood pressure. If your blood pressure falls too low, it's an indication you could be seriously ill. If your blood pressure goes to zero, obviously you're dead. So, if the economy goes to zero, it means no one is using cash. At that point, we would be on a barter system.

Currently the economy is at a point where interest rates are very low and is a sign the economy is stable and remaining healthy. If the economy resumes a healthy resurgence, we will find interest rates firming up. This would hurt bonds and help stocks. This is when bond investors need to beware.

We experienced in the 70s and 80s high volatility and big swings from an eight prime rate to a 20 prime rate and back down to a six prime. Those days are over. During the 90s decade and the first 10 years of the next century, we will experience an interest rate pattern similar to that of the 40s and 50s where interest rates stayed reasonably calm and flat. In essence, the potential for rates to decline is minimal at this juncture, but the potential for their increase to the highs of the 70s and 80s is also minimal. The current environment is almost opposite that of the last 20 years. It is my belief that the trend will be for interest rates to slowly increase over the next two decades.

What? No Free Lunch?

Now, we've discussed the historical perspectives of the stock market and the rationale for long-term investing, including doing your research, diversifying, forecasting, using a system and having the discipline to adhere to it through thick and thin and how world events affect the market. But, I know there are still those who expect to automatically be successful investors without really trying.

My last words to those individuals are that you are not entitled to have a successful investment portfolio on a whim. Fate or luck may play a part, but there is truly no such thing as a free lunch. The bear will claw you or the bull will gore you if you don't take a responsible, systematic approach to your financial future.

How to Accumulate Wealth: Bypassing the Human Nature Flaw

"Gosh, I would have been better off in a CD."
—A common investor complaint

The market was jumping at the end of 1976. It had just enjoyed two fruitful years, but as I evaluated my clients' portfolio performance, I was hit between the eyes with dismal results. I

---

just couldn't figure it out. Something was real screwy here.

As I continued to analyze and compare products I was recommending to my clients, I began to realize that most of my clients were not tolerant of any risk whatsoever and should have been in the safest, most conservative of investment vehicles.

Now, about this time, the securities industry's most competitive product was the bank certificate of deposit (CD). Their popularity was due to the comfort factor of the investment. Many conservative investors (and who doesn't claim to be conservative?) would continue to ask what other types of investments could be purchased that would offer the same security, safety, and comfort level as the CD.

Well, in all honesty, there was not much out there. And I put a lot of my clients in CDs because I really believed in them. Still do. And when all was said and done, it was my opinion that we really couldn't beat the CDs. But something new was coming down the pike during this period of deregulation in the 70s. Something uncomplicated, solid, and backed by the richest organization in the world: the single premium deferred annuity was introduced to Wall Street by the insurance industry.

Safest Product in the U.S.

I pulled out my calculator and began working the figures and looking at the facts and the literature that was available to me. It seemed to have all of the features of a CD: preservation of capital, adjustability of interest rates, ability to stagger the quantity—plus, the most beautiful aspect of all— as the capital grows, it compounds tax-free. The SPDA is the single smartest, safest, and easiest accumulation investment product in America.

One of the misconceptions people have about deferred annuities (and most other tax-deferred vehicles, for that matter) is that at age 65 they'll have to pay taxes on all the capital they've accumulated. Well, that's baloney. There's no law that says you have to pull your money out at age 59, 65 or even 70. However, if you withdraw your cash before age 59-1/2, you pay a 10 percent excise tax just as you do with IRAs, 40lKs, Keoghs, and other various qualified retirement accounts. There is a surrender fee, similar to the CD withdrawal, if you cash in the first five to seven years or so.

Insurance companies holding the annuities require that investors who haven't touched their investment by around age 85 must start withdrawing their money and paying taxes on it. But, I suggest if you don't want to pay the taxes during your lifetime you can arrange to have a younger member of the family be the annuitant.

It's OK with Uncle Sam

Now, let's talk more about what tax-deferred means to us. Tax-deferred investments are true tax shelters, approved by Congress, that are straightforward, legal, and effective. Deferring your taxes allows you to put more money to work, which, being free of the tax burden, allows it to grow at a faster rate. And you may find that you can defer taxes on your capital sum indefinitely, as I pointed out earlier.

Let's take a closer look at the vital feature of compounding, and what effect it has on your invested money. Table 7-1 provides an example:

At 30 years, even if A took the most costly option and paid 30 percent taxes in full on his capital, he would have $70,438.20 which is $17,438 more, after tax, than B.

Table 7-1

A compounds $10,000 at 8% tax-deferred
B compounds $10,000 at 8% taxable at 28%

	10 years	*20 years*	*30 years*
A Deferred	$21,589	$46,609	$100,626
B Taxable	17,500	30,000	53,000

Table 7-2 is another example.

At 30 years, even if C took his most costly option and paid 30% taxes in full on his capital, he would have $95,172 which is $8,504 more, after tax, than D.

It's really quite astounding, isn't it?

Now, back to the withdrawal aspect of the annuity product. After you retire, if you need income, you could take your money out in monthly payments which are not all taxed, because part of the distribution can be considered principal.

SPDAs are set up so that you can invest as little as $2,500. This feature makes it very attractive to small investors. In my estimation, this product is the most efficient and

---

Table 7-2

C and D are able to save $100 per month. C saves $100 per month compounded at 8% annual tax deferred. D saves $100 per month compounded at 8% annually subject to 20% income tax.

	10 years	*20 years*	*30 years*
C Deferred	$17,400	$54,96	$135,960
D Taxable	13,718	39,228	86,668

---

simple device available to the investing public because it provides the ideal accumulation system.

An example of its efficiency is that if you put $10,000 in a bank CD paying 8 percent and if it's not rolled over, your $10,000 could soon dwindle down because it is too accessible to you. But a $10,000 annuity is more difficult to access—it's not attached to your checkbook. So as far as human nature is concerned, you aren't as tempted to peel off layers of your capital. Most people tend to put their annuity accounts aside and out of their minds, like a retirement account.

Here is a good example: I put a client in a $10,000 annuity on May 9, 1984. Its value was $19,295 on August 31, 1989. This means the account had risen 11.62 percent annually for the last eight years. And remember, these years included the sky-high interest rates and the extremely low interest rates—all throughout these roller coaster years, the account was never at risk. This rate of return is exceeded only by the stock market returns.

Annuities are excellent investments for individuals in their 30s or 40s as part of their retirement planning. If you are near retirement, you'll find them a safe way to earn current yields, usually over bank rates, too. In addition to a company pension plan and social security, SPDAs make an attractive addition to your financial planning equation. Obviously, the earlier you invest, the greater the compound effect of tax deferral on growth of capital. The longer you defer taxes, the harder your money works.

Unfortunately, as remarkable as this product is, there still is public ignorance and market resistance to it. Many times, I'll mention the word "annuity" to a client and he or she will say, "Oh, no, that's for someone who is retired." Or, "What are you, an insurance salesmen?"

Well, take a look at your tax returns. On the line below your reported gross income you have to write in the amount of interest you are paying—for instance, the amount you have earned from your savings account. If that is a sizable figure, relative to your situation, you can arrange to remove all of those dollars showing up in that column. Let me give you an example:

Let's say you earn $50,000 a year and you've managed to accumulate $100,000 in the bank. You report a 5 percent or $5,000 interest to the IRS. Why don't you put $80,000 in a deferred annuity and keep $20,000 in the bank? You can get 6 percent on the $80,000, which is $4,800 and not have to report it on the 1099 form because you don't receive 1099s on tax-deferred accumulating accounts.

> **"Annuities are excellent investments for individuals in their 30s or 40s as part of their retirement planning."**

Now, since many of us are skeptical beings, we might say, "Well, there must be a few strings attached. It sounds too good to be true." Well, of course. Most everything in life is a compromise. As I said earlier, there will be a withdrawal fee, very much like the bank CD penalties. For example, the bank says they'll give you, say, 5 percent interest on your $100,000, but you can't touch the capital for three years. The insurance company says the same thing in essence. But their charges are very liberal. You won't wipe out your accrued interest; you'll just pay a 5 percent or so "service charge" if you take out in excess of 10 percent a year. Here's an example:

You invest $100,000 at 6 percent in an annuity. A year goes by and something happens and you have to take out the $6,000 interest paid for an emergency or whatever. Your $6,000 withdrawal has no penalty because usually you can withdraw 10 percent per year without any service charges. Now, let's say you need $20,000. You can take the $6,000 interest earned and $4,000 of the capital without a service charge. The insurance company will charge you a 5 percent or $500 service charge on the additional $10,000 of capital you withdrew of the $20,000. Now, there are taxes due.

I say, so what if it's taxable? The $20,000 that you needed was probably for a medical problem, catastrophic loss, business loss, or something of that nature—which will probably be a tax write-off anyway. So, the tax will be minor and won't make a big difference to you.

You may be thinking, "What happens when I reach age 65 and withdraw cash for living expenses. Won't that be taxable income?" Yes, but what's wrong with that? Let's say you were an executive of a company and your salary was $80,000 when you retired. Your benefits could be $21,000 from Social Security and a $30,000 pension. Now you have $51,000 income per year. Your tax bracket now drops. If you withdraw from your annuity, you are in a lower tax bracket. Or, let's say you want a deal so that when you retire you can have the same amount of pension income as you had in your last working years' salary, so your bracket will stay high. Well, I ask you, what's the problem here? And you'll say, "When I want to take the money out, I'll pay the same taxes on it and I really haven't saved anything." Well, I say be reasonable. It sounds like a bunch of baloney to me. If you have an $80,000 income at work and when you retire you have an $80,000 income, why are you taking money out of your account, anyway? You probably don't need it. If your pension resources are giving you $80,000, why are you spending all of your savings? Unless, of course, you are frivolous and can't live on $80,000—which is fine for some people, I guess.

The point I'm trying to drive home is that investors usually never end up taking money from these accounts unless it is for a dire emergency or the like. And, if it is an emergency, there's usually a tax deduction involved.

Now for the ultimate pessimist. Let's say the pessimist is in a 30 percent tax bracket. And he says, "What if, 20 years down the road, I am in a 50 percent tax bracket?" Then he says, "Gosh, I shouldn't have invested in this annuity because all the time I've been deferring tax, I could have been paying less on it." Well, that's a great argument if you're looking for outlandish excuses not to invest. But why resort to rhetoric? Take your calculator out and what you'll find is that, because of reinvestment of the interest and the tax re-compounding, you now have 80 percent more than you would have otherwise. So even if you're paying a 50 percent tax, you're 30 percent better off.

It All Adds Up to Profits

That's what I love about this business. It can be so simple once you use your calculator. All of the rhetoric is just hot air. Investing in an annuity is not theory, not opinion, or salesmanship. It's arithmetic, pure and simple. And it all adds up to big profits for you, the investor.

I think more and more people are thinking about saving more and spending less these days. I think you'll see a tremendous use of the IRA, deferred annuities, 401Ks, vehicles that compound tax-free. It's like a forced savings account.

In addition to deferred annuities, corporate pensions IRAs and 401Ks, there are many other plans available including Keoghs, Simplified Employee Pensions (SEP), profit-sharing, single premium life insurance. They contain many helpful options which include deducting your contribution from your current income tax, matching funds contributed by your employer, and flexible contributions. Other options include emergency withdrawals, vesting rights, selecting and/or changing your investment goals as well as voluntary after-tax contributions that nevertheless earn tax-deferred.

There are even more options for when and how you may withdraw funds, receive a lump-sum, roll over a lump sum to an IRA, take income from your capital, leave your capital to your spouse, your estate, or to named beneficiaries.

Back to Basics

But, let's get back to those competitive products: the certificate of deposit (CDs) and the single premium deferred annuity (SPDA). These investments are hard to beat. They require almost no effort. All you have to do is put your money down. They should do what they say they will do. Unfortunately, most people are chasing the impossible dream; they think they can do better than these guaranteed CD-type investments without really trying.

Historically speaking, CDs are adjustable. Typically, people buy CDs one year at a time. And every 12 months, they renew. If interest rates rise, they ride the yields. Now the yield curve will fall, as we know, because interest rates fluctuate. If you bought long-term one- to five-year CDs before rates start dropping, you have locked in a rate of return that is higher than rates being earned by other invest- ors. On the other hand, if interest rates are low and are expected to rise, it's best to use short-term CDs. This way, you can take advantage of rising interest rates when your CDs mature. For example, suppose you buy a three-month CD when rates are low. You will be able to reinvest your cash in a new and hopefully higher-rate CD at the end of just three months. Remember, we always know what inter- est rates will do: they will either rise, fall, or stay the same. Even if you have no idea which way rates are headed, you can assemble a portfolio of CDs that have different maturi- ties. Table 7-3 is an example of a $50,000 portfolio.

This portfolio is built upon the assumption that interest rates will rise in the near term. If you believe interest rates will fall in the near term, you will probably want to lengthen the time periods to lock in your return.

Also, you should know that there is no current tax on a CD that you buy for a retirement plan. Since there is no current tax dilution of interest earned in a plan, your nest egg will grow at a much faster rate. The tax is deferred until you start making withdrawals from the retirement plan, much like the annuity we discussed earlier.

Table 7-3

$10,000 CD	30 days	Short-term interest rate
$10,000 CD	60 days	Short-term interest rate + .5%
$25,000 CD	6 months	Short-term interest rate + .8%
$ 5,000 CD	1 year	Short-term interest rate +1.5%

Another important aspect of the CD transaction is your banker. The banker wants a depositor to put $100,000 into just one large CD because the odds are great that a good number of depositors who buy a term CD in large blocks will need the money during the specified time frame and have to "bust" the CD. Then the bank can retroactively reduce the interest to practically zero. Let's say you opened a $100,000 CD for a 10-year period. You are in the eighth

> **"Statistically, most investments do not outperform the interest paid over the guaranteed capital value of the CD-type instruments."**

year and you need a large amount of cash. If the rate was 8 percent, the banker can reduce this to 5.25 percent for the last seven years. In other words, if you break the terms of the CD, you revert back to the passbook rate of, say, 5 percent. And, you may be taking away from the capital at that point! So, if the bank overpaid you in interest, instead of receiving $100,000, you might get $80,000 of your original capital. Of course, the banker knows that would be financial suicide, so he suggests you borrow the money from the bank. And that's why banks prefer to have large CDs.

Another positive aspect of the CD for the investor is that it can adapt to the environment. I maintain that if your investment cannot adapt to the environment—just like anything else on this planet—it gets wiped out. And, believe me, this is exactly what happens to many investments on Wall Street.

The fact of the matter is that the criticism most often heard about Wall Street investments is, "Gosh, I would have been better off in a CD!" It is a well-known fact, by those experienced on Wall Street that, statistically, most investments do not outperform the interest paid over the guaranteed capital value of the CD-type instruments. This is not necessarily due to the nature of the product itself, but to human nature flaws. The interest paid to you on a CD depends upon current money market conditions and the length of time you agree to leave your money on deposit. Generally speaking, the longer you keep your money on deposit, the higher the interest rate. It also depends upon how often the money is compounded. The more frequently interest is compounded, the more interest you will accumulate. Let me give you an example:

Suppose you put $10,000 in a three-year, 7 percent CD. If interest is compounded annually, you will earn $2,250 in interest. If it's compounded monthly, you'll earn $2,329 and with daily compounding your interest will be $2,336.

With a CD, you always know how much money you have invested, how much it is earning, and how much you can withdraw at any time. This is truly a worry-free investment.

Only Two Rules to Remember

The power of fixed, guaranteed investments like these is not only their adjustability to the interest cycles, but the elimination of errors caused by the human nature tendency to buy high-flying investments at the peak of their popularity only to sell when they decline, creating a loss in the portfolio. CDs and SPDAs preserve capital. They remind me of the adage: Rule 1—Don't lose money. Rule 2—Don't forget Rule 1.

Both systems have time in their favor. The SPDA uses an additional leveraging system of tax-deferral allowing no tax burden during the crucial accumulation phase. CDs can accomplish this when they are used within tax deferred account strategies like your IRA or 401K.

The Deferred Account Plus! Stock Investing

Now factor what you should have learned from the bond and stock chapters—nothing outperforms the returns given by equities or stocks over time. Consider, for example, that within a 20-year cycle, 100 percent of the time stocks have performed better than any other investment alternative. The success rate of stocks even in five-year cycles is almost always consistently better than corporate bonds, for example. Think of the power of placing stocks within a systematic approach such as your IRA, 401K, or mutual fund accounts on a long-term basis as you would with your CDs or SPDAs. Now you can harness the power of time, stock performance, discipline, patience—and eliminate the human nature flaw.

You now can control your economic fate, and not leave it to luck. This is a very powerful tool to possess. The fascinating part of the math is that the most significant aspect is not the importance of yearly performance that all Wall Street dwells on. If your portfolio makes 9-11 percent in the long run, the impact on performance is dwarfed by the value added by time and the re-investment compounding factors.

Study the columns in the exhibit by *Investor's Digest* (Table 7-4) where 10 percent is used, which is below the historical rate of return of 12 percent for stocks, and lower than the all-time best mutual funds.

Table 7-4 Early Start IRA: How $6,750 Grows to Over $1 Million

This table shows four ways to accumulate approximately $1,000,000 in an IRA by age 65. Investor A contributes $2,000 at the beginning of each year for forty years (ages 26-65); Investor B, $2,000 a year for only seven years (19-25); Investor C, $2,000 a year for only five years (age 14-18); and Investor D smaller sums still from age 8 through 13. Finally, Investor E shows the IRA growth achieved by making all of these contributions at every age from 8 to 65.

Age	INVESTOR A Contribution	Year-End Value	INVESTOR B Contribution	Year-End Value	INVESTOR C Contribution	Year-End Value	INVESTOR D Contribution	Year-End Value	INVESTOR E Contribution	Year-End Value
8	-0-	-0-	-0-	-0-	-0-	-0-	500	550	500	550
9	-0-	-0-	-0-	-0-	-0-	-0-	750	1,430	750	1,430
10	-0-	-0-	-0-	-0-	-0-	-0-	1,000	2,673	1,000	2,673
11	-0-	-0-	-0-	-0-	-0-	-0-	1,250	4,315	1,250	4,315
12	-0-	-0-	-0-	-0-	-0-	-0-	1,500	6,397	1,500	6,397
13	-0-	-0-	-0-	-0-	-0-	-0-	1,750	8,962	1,750	8,962
14	-0-	-0-	-0-	-0-	2,000	2,200	-0-	9,858	2,000	12,058
15	-0-	-0-	-0-	-0-	2,000	4,620	-0-	10,843	2,000	15,463
16	-0-	-0-	-0-	-0-	2,000	7,282	-0-	11,928	2,000	19,210
17	-0-	-0-	-0-	-0-	2,000	10,210	-0-	13,121	2,000	23,331
18	-0-	-0-	-0-	-0-	2,000	13,431	-0-	14,433	2,000	27,864
19	-0-	-0-	2,000	2,200	-0-	14,774	-0-	15,876	2,000	32,850
20	-0-	-0-	2,000	4,620	-0-	16,252	-0-	17,463	2,000	38,335
21	-0-	-0-	2,000	7,282	-0-	17,877	-0-	19,210	2,000	44,369
22	-0-	-0-	2,000	10,210	-0-	19,665	-0-	21,131	2,000	51,006
23	-0-	-0-	2,000	13,431	-0-	21,631	-0-	23,244	2,000	58,306
24	-0-	-0-	2,000	16,974	-0-	23,794	-0-	25,568	2,000	66,337
25	-0-	-0-	2,000	20,872	-0-	26,174	-0-	28,125	2,000	75,170
26	2,000	2,200	-0-	22,959	-0-	28,791	-0-	30,938	2,000	84,888
27	2,000	4,620	-0-	25,255	-0-	31,670	-0-	34,031	2,000	95,576
28	2,000	7,282	-0-	27,780	-0-	34,837	-0-	37,434	2,000	107,334
29	2,000	10,210	-0-	30,558	-0-	38,321	-0-	41,178	2,000	120,267
30	2,000	13,431	-0-	33,614	-0-	42,153	-0-	45,296	2,000	134,494
31	2,000	16,974	-0-	36,976	-0-	46,368	-0-	49,825	2,000	150,143
32	2,000	20,872	-0-	40,673	-0-	51,005	-0-	54,808	2,000	167,358

Age	Invest	Earnings		Earnings		Earnings		Earnings	Invest	Earnings
33	2,000	25,159	-0-	44,741	-0-	56,106	-0-	60,289	2,000	186,294
34	2,000	29,875	-0-	49,215	-0-	61,716	-0-	66,317	2,000	207,123
35	2,000	35,062	-0-	54,136	-0-	67,888	-0-	72,949	2,000	230,035
36	2,000	40,769	-0-	59,550	-0-	74,676	-0-	80,244	2,000	255,239
37	2,000	47,045	-0-	65,505	-0-	82,144	-0-	88,269	2,000	282,963
38	2,000	53,950	-0-	72,055	-0-	90,359	-0-	97,095	2,000	313,459
39	2,000	61,545	-0-	79,261	-0-	99,394	-0-	106,805	2,000	347,005
40	2,000	69,899	-0-	87,187	-0-	109,334	-0-	117,485	2,000	383,905
41	2,000	79,089	-0-	95,905	-0-	120,267	-0-	129,234	2,000	424,496
42	2,000	89,198	-0-	105,496	-0-	132,294	-0-	142,157	2,000	469,145
43	2,000	100,318	-0-	116,045	-0-	145,523	-0-	156,373	2,000	518,269
44	2,000	112,550	-0-	127,650	-0-	160,076	-0-	172,010	2,000	572,286
45	2,000	126,005	-0-	140,415	-0-	176,083	-0-	189,211	2,000	631,714
46	2,000	140,805	-0-	154,456	-0-	193,692	-0-	208,133	2,000	697,086
47	2,000	157,086	-0-	169,902	-0-	213,061	-0-	228,946	2,000	768,995
48	2,000	174,995	-0-	186,892	-0-	234,367	-0-	251,840	2,000	848,094
49	2,000	194,694	-0-	205,581	-0-	257,803	-0-	277,024	2,000	935,103
50	2,000	216,364	-0-	226,140	-0-	283,358	-0-	304,727	2,000	1,030,814
51	2,000	240,200	-0-	248,754	-0-	311,942	-0-	335,209	2,000	1,136,095
52	2,000	266,420	-0-	273,629	-0-	343,136	-0-	368,719	2,000	1,251,905
53	2,000	295,262	-0-	300,992	-0-	377,450	-0-	405,591	2,000	1,379,295
54	2,000	326,988	-0-	331,091	-0-	415,195	-0-	446,150	2,000	1,519,425
55	2,000	361,887	-0-	364,200	-0-	456,715	-0-	490,766	2,000	1,673,567
56	2,000	400,276	-0-	400,620	-0-	502,386	-0-	539,842	2,000	1,843,124
57	2,000	442,503	-0-	440,682	-0-	552,625	-0-	593,826	2,000	2,029,636
58	2,000	488,953	-0-	484,750	-0-	607,887	-0-	653,209	2,000	2,234,800
59	2,000	540,049	-0-	533,225	-0-	668,676	-0-	718,530	2,000	2,460,480
60	2,000	596,254	-0-	586,548	-0-	735,543	-0-	790,383	2,000	2,708,728
61	2,000	658,079	-0-	645,203	-0-	809,098	-0-	869,421	2,000	2,981,800
62	2,000	726,087	-0-	709,723	-0-	890,007	-0-	956,363	2,000	3,282,180
63	2,000	800,896	-0-	780,695	-0-	979,008	-0-	1,052,000	2,000	3,612,598
64	2,000	883,185	-0-	858,765	-0-	1,076,909	-0-	1,157,200	2,000	3,976,058
65	2,000	973,704	-0-	944,641	-0-	1,184,600	-0-	1,272,930	2,000	4,375,864
Less Total Invested:		(80,000)		(14,000)		(10,000)		(6,750)		(110,750)
Equals Net Earnings:		893,704		930,641		1,174,600		1,266,170		4,265,114
Money Grew:		11-fold		66-fold		117-fold		188-fold		38-fold

SOURCE: Investor's Digest, 3471 N. Federal, Fort Lauderdale, FL 33306, Telephone: (800) 442-9000, 1 year, 12 months, $29.

For example, the Templeton Growth Fund advertisement (Figure 7-1) shows $10,000 invested for 53 years is worth $1,668,675.

Which mutual fund will be the best in the next 53 years? What if you invest a total of $6,750 like Investor D in two or three no-load equity funds that averaged 10 percent? You would end up with $1,272,930. If, instead, you invested $10,000, you would have done 30 percent better making your investment worth $1,700,000. Not bad for not having picked the best fund and only getting average equity performance!

Now, do the best of all worlds. Look at Investor E and eliminate human nature, systematically compounding tax-free and systematically invest $2,000 per year with discipline. $4,000,000 has accumulated in 57 years. In 42 years, the investment is worth $1,030,814 at $2,000 per year. These are some pretty astounding figures!

Let's take it a step further. What would happen if you elected to contribute the maximum to your 401K, and $2,000 per year to your IRA and supplement those two with a variable annuity which is a tax-deferred growth mutual fund equity account. Among the three accounts you are saving almost $10,000 a year and could accumulate about $5,000,000 within a 40-year period of time!

The key here is your ability to save that much of your paycheck. I understand that's the difficult part, but here is where reading magazines like *Money* or the *Kiplinger Letter* or even *Consumer's Digest* will be helpful. You always want to look for ways to save money in your budget by being cost-conscious. Take your savings and hoard it.

My main point is to use the accumulation, tax-deferred equity systems that bypass the human nature flaw.

Figure 7-1   Time Works with Stocks

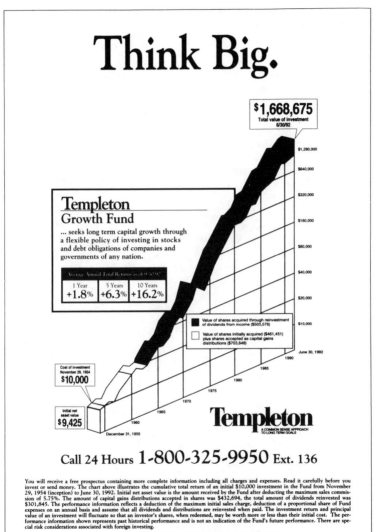

8

Follow the Yellow Brick Road: Which Wizard Is Which?

So far, you've learned why stocks out-perform bonds and why bonds are considered to be a poor investment. You've also learned about alternative safe investments such as annuities and CDs as well as which debt instruments to avoid. Chapter 5 outlined deceptive marketing techniques and terminology in marketing materials and pointed out—step-by-step—which prospectus information is critical to study before investing. With all this ammunition in your knowledge arsenal, you are now ready to step into the world of securities. Right?

Wrong!

To my way of thinking, many books fall short by about two or three chapters. Where is the personal guidance you need as you take that giant step (or your re-entry) into the investment universe? Do you simply look in the Yellow Pages for a financial planner or stockbroker and walk into their office and plunk your money down? Or do you look for a discount firm and do your own trading? How about picking an aggressive portfolio manager who boasts the highest performance for the year? Maybe you should visit the library and check out the Weisenberger directory of mutual funds and pick one from the thousands listed!

Think about it. You're really just beginning. The next few chapters will help you understand which financial professionals can help you and why you should work with them.

What's in a Name?

First let's set the record straight about titles and what each one means to you. Many brokerage firms give their own brokers special titles to set them apart from competitive firms' brokers and to add prestige to their positions. For example—customer's man, account executive, financial consultant, investment consultant, securities counselor, and financial advisor—all mean the same thing: full service stockbroker. If you hear the term "registered representative," you are also talking about a stockbroker. An RR is the formal title as all brokers are "registered and licensed professionals" with their firms. A full service stockbroker is regulated by the Securities and Exchange Commission and supervised by the top management of his stock exchange-member brokerage firm.

> **" All investors—small, medium and large—profit from good, solid investment advice."**

Now, the title "financial planner" is very nebulous and can mean just about anything these days. There are no licenses needed for this title. Anyone can hang a shingle with this designation, although many individuals (mostly stockbrokers and insurance brokers) take courses to become Certified Financial Planners (CFPs). Financial planners cannot sell securities unless they are Series 7-licensed registered representatives (stockbrokers).

Portfolio advisors, portfolio managers, investment advisors, money managers—these are all generic terms for the registered investment advisor (RIA). Many are chartered financial analysts (CFAs). These professionals analyze the markets and manage your investment portfolios on a day-to-day basis. These professionals are the Rolls-Royces of the investment community. Now, a new group of professionals are emerging who work closely with these investment advisors (or money managers). They are called Investment Management Consultants and are a new breed of stockbrokers who work with individuals and small to mid-sized companies in search of money managers to personally oversee their assets. These investment management consultants add value to the brokerage account/client by locating the manager, analyzing, and monitoring his performance and servicing the client on a frequent basis. It is interesting to note that IMCs are able to eliminate the perceived conflict of interest that occurs in buy-and-sell transactions, since the manager, not the broker (who is on commission) makes the decisions on when and how often to make transactions.

All investors—small, medium and large—profit from good, solid investment advice. The proper information from knowledgeable and experienced investment professionals can help you set realistic goals, make financial plans, and bring discipline to your financial affairs. In turn, you will achieve safety and increase your net worth and/or your income.

Fee or Free?

I feel that the best financial advice should be free. Think about it. If a financial planner knows what he or she is doing, you will get the best investment advice for the least cost. It's their job to do just that for you. Better yet, the fees owed the planner should be paid for by the investment return, not the investor. If you knew what I did about fees and commissions being charged by the "financial planning" industry (and I use the term loosely, with all due respect to the bona fide hard-working professionals out there) you would know that you don't have to pay excessive fees and commissions to get the best financial planning, which should, in turn, maximize your return on capital.

Financial planners can charge you a fee to analyze your financial affairs and provide you with a set of recommendations. Now, you could find yourself paying for recommendations you don't like or agree with. Why pay for a large, bound book full of re-organized, re-stated information that is already clearly stated in three basic forms:

1. Your 1040 federal income tax form.

2. Your employment benefits package.

3. Your personal financial statement of assets and liabilities.

To further illustrate, your insurance coverage, brokerage accounts, and real estate holdings are all reflected on your 1040 and financial statement. Your corporate buy/sell agreement is part of your benefits package or financial statement.

A planner will charge either a flat fee, an hourly fee or percentage of assets fee to work up this plan for you. There will more than likely be an annual advisory fee for reviewing your results and in many cases an implementation fee and/or a timing fee for shifting investments to meet market conditions, or your changing goals.

Let me take you through a typical financial planning scenario. You visit your planner bringing with you your past tax filings, financial statement, and job information such as salary, tenure, and pension fund details. You supply all cost of living expenses, family budget, children's educational requirements, parental care, and future goals. After completing a lengthy questionnaire, including questions about market risk, you will receive a computer printout or written plan with investment recommendations. The charges for this service can be a flat fee starting at $500 and going as high as $10,000, or an hourly rate of $100-$200, or the percentage of assets to be invested fee.

The plan could be of such a general nature that it would require an implementation fee to put it in effect in addition to possible timing fees to keep abreast of market conditions as I mentioned above. If the planner sells you a mutual fund, he could make an up-front sales commission of between 4 and 8 percent. If you buy a limited partnership, the commissions can run as high as 10 percent. The limited partnership, like the mutual fund, has its management fees and transaction commissions within the management of the portfolio. The planner might offer the timing program for another 1 percent management fee on top of it all.

Add up the transaction and investment advisory/management fees and you get five to seven layered costs. If you need a CPA or a lawyer, add two more costs. Historically, the financial planner would earn all fees and commissions at the point of sale and have no economic vested interest in actual performance over time. The majority of financial planners are paid primarily by commissions and/or fees.

Know Who You Are Dealing with, or—No Deal!

Unfortunately, the financial planning industry has had its share of unscrupulous planners who abuse the title and wreak financial havoc on unsophisticated investors. The biggest problem is the conflict between the planner's role as a seller of financial products and his role as an adviser. Many times the promise of financial planning is objective advice, but, all too often, the reality is a sales pitch cloaked in the *trappings* of objectivity.

The major federal law affecting financial planners, the Investment Advisers Act of 1940, doesn't really regulate planners at all. It does little more than require all investment advisers to register with the U.S. Securities and Exchange

Commission and provide details on their educational background.

If you decide to work with a financial planner, here are a few guidelines I recommend for choosing a good one:

1. Interview at least three professionals who are recommended by friends or business associates.

2. Ask to see plans the planner has developed for other clients.

3. Insist on references—at least three—from long-term clients and talk to each of them at length. Ask for the names of lawyers and accountants they do business with, too.

4. Make sure you understand the fee schedule in advance. Professional planners will disclose how much they are making from any product they advise you to buy.

5. Get all plans and recommendations in writing and keep detailed notes of conversations with your planner.

6. Review the planner's work periodically to see if it is meeting your original goals and suits your comfort level.

7. At the very least, insist on a planner who carries the Certified Financial Planner (CFP) designation issued by the International Association for Financial Planning in Atlanta. If the planner carries the ChFC designation, he is a well-trained life insurance agent and is likely to sell a lot of it—to you.

8. To check on any securities violations, civil complaints, or criminal actions, contact the North Amer-

ican Securities Administrators Association in Washington, D.C., for information on state records. Their number is 1-800-289-9999.

This is a good time to remind you that low cost financial planning alternatives are available through certain accounting firms. For example, some of the big eight accounting firms will prepare a personal financial analysis that covers net worth, tax strategies, investment strategies, projections for education and retirement savings, insurance evaluation, stock options advice, and limited estate planning. On average you can expect to pay about $500 for this service.

A rule of thumb is don't pay more than 1 percent of your investment assets and income for a plan.

Talk is Not "Cheap"

To get the best investment and financial advice the cost must work for you. If the cost is cheap, you are likely to get superficial information and be ill-advised. Your investments could be risky, poor performers or, worse, even losers. On the other hand, if your costs are excessive, the returns on your investment program will probably suffer the weight of these costs.

The basic costs of investing are the brokerage fees and commissions you pay to buy and sell stocks, which are typically called transaction costs. Management fees are paid to the investment advisor (money manager) on all professionally managed accounts such as mutual funds, limited partnerships, bond funds, and other types of securities investments. Transaction and management fees are unavoidable. A typical investment advisor fee is around 1 percent. This is charged annually and is based on the value of your portfolio. Obviously, the investment advisor wants the value of your portfolio to increase since the more you earn, the more he earns. Also, the advisor wants the commission cost to stay low, so the performance figures are better. Historically, managed stock accounts cost less than 2 percent a year in stock commission transactions and 1 percent or less for the management fee. Think about it: You have professional investment advice and have covered the transaction costs, plus receive the services of a full service stockbroker.

To further illustrate, the management services fee of 1 percent and transaction costs from commissions sometimes are "wrapped" into one fee, commonly known as the "wrap fee." You can be offered a wrap fee of 3 percent or, for larger accounts, a discounted fee of 2 percent. This is called "bundling" because the management fee and the commissions are charged to the account quarterly—but at the annual rate.

Now, here's something else you need to be aware of. Banks are now offering wrap fees of 1 percent versus our 3 percent. How is this possible? It all seems very logical on the surface to choose the 1 percent over the 3 percent, but what they don't tell you in their advertising is this: The bank is using a managed pool account. These pooled funds are managed by their choice of investment management firm. The management firm will charge the pooled funds a management fee. The pooled funds will pay the commissions on the transactions, just like a "no load" (or no-commission) mutual fund. Then, the bank charges you merely "1 percent." This is no deal. Why not just invest in a mutual fund? Even the most conservative bank knows how to use Madison Avenue marketing techniques to compare apples to jalapenos!

A discussion of fees is not complete without covering additional costs you may incur if you buy a mutual fund.

There are myriad ways of looking at these figures and volumes have been written about it, but simply stated, you will always pay "something" for the services of a professionally managed mutual fund, even if they tout the fact that no commissions are charged. A no-load—or no commission—fund may elect to charge you an exit or a sales charge when you sell your fund. Also, an annual management fee can be charged for expenses, advertising and general administration. Other types of funds can charge as high as 8 percent for up front sales commissions. Now, I'm not saying this is wrong, but you need to ask questions and be sure to read the fine print as I recommended in Chapter 5 so there are no surprises down the line in your investment program.

Now, let's talk about the full service broker and what the advantages are of working with this type of professional.

Service—The Most Important Product

A full service stockbroker provides you with financial and investment advice, planning, goal setting, on-going consultation, and service and guidance vis-à-vis various market conditions. A full service broker can provide research as done by the firm and can recommend from the over 400 investment products that are available. This service is done for the transaction costs plus a small percentage fee to an investment advisor, if you opt for a managed account. The total costs to you are approximately 2-3 percent per year of your asset value.

Your full service broker encourages you to call or come in for consultations or follow-ups at any time; this is the added value you get for the commission you pay. This is a valuable service which helps keep you on track with your financial goals during difficult markets and especially when the human nature flaws of greed and fear set in. Of course, you may decide to use a discount broker who charges a slightly lower commission, but he offers no advice, financial plan, or consulting and investment management. Don't attempt to use a discount broker unless you are a sophisticated investor and watch the markets carefully, or already have a particular stock in mind that you want and don't need any advice or guidance on. These brokers are great for the do-it-yourselfers.

In the case of the full-service stockbroker, he, too, will need your 1040 form, your financial statement, your employment benefits package, and any other pertinent family information, just as the financial planner does. Now, once a broker understands your finances, the question is, can this broker help you? Can your financial outlook be improved?

Here's what a full service stockbroker might advise for you in a typical scenario. After discussing your estate value by looking at your corporate benefits and financial statement, you might be advised to update or change your will. This is information you would normally pay for if you visited an attorney. Then the broker might notice from your 1040 that you are in a high income tax bracket. Plus, you have several CDs earning interest and generating reportable income on your taxes. The broker may then recommend deferred annuities, for example. You can replace your CDs with annuities and the insurance company will pay the broker his commission, not you. Next, maybe you have growth mutual funds that should go into stocks. The broker will evaluate which mutual funds will best meet your financial goals. The fund could be no-load (no-commission) or a load fund. Be careful, however, before making your decision on choosing between load and no-load, because oftentimes the no-load funds have hidden charges, such as sales, advertising and administrative fees that can total more than a broker's commission!

In my opinion, one of the most valuable reasons to have a full-service stockbroker or investment management consultant in your back pocket is that he can recommend the best investment advisor for your funds, if you do opt for professionally-managed service. There is no front-end sales charges or hidden back-end (withdrawal) charges. And as I see it, the stockbroker has no conflict of interest with the commissions being generated because he cannot make any changes to the portfolio. This is the ideal person to have on your side.

Fees being what they are, you still need to consider that the performance return you net is above the free rate of return available at your local bank. Otherwise you don't need any experts.

Consider Your Options

Let's take a look at some comparison examples of a hypothetical financial plan recommended by both a financial planner and a full-service broker. Say you are a 40-year old male and have just inherited $500,000 from your favorite aunt. For $5,000 the financial planner designs and implements an investment plan. The planner recommends $300,000 be invested in several diversified mutual funds and $200,000 in limited partnerships. There will be up front sales charges on the mutual funds of 6 percent and on the partnerships, 10 percent. The total fees are $43,000. The planner then charges a 1 percent timing fee to shift the mutual funds to meet the market conditions and charges $500 for an annual review and consultation. So far you have been charged $46,500.

In both the partnerships and the mutual funds, a general administration and management fee is charged and the investment managers of the funds receive an annual percentage fee on assets. The planner, like an insurance licensed full-service broker, could sell you $1,000,000 in additional life insurance to cover additional estate taxes. Commissions of $5,000-$20,000 can be generated depending upon the type of policy. A new will is needed and an accountant should be consulted for tax and estate calculations. Fees are charged by the attorneys and CPAs for this as well.

So far this year, your total costs could be anywhere between $51,000 and $66,000 if you work with this particular plan. Now let's take a look at the full-service stockbroker and what you would be paying in fees for the same type of service.

After understanding your financial status and goals, the full-service stockbroker will recommend that your $500,000 be invested in a diversified and balanced portfolio managed by an independent investment advisor. There will be no excessive turn-over or what we call "churning" of your account. There is no fee for the plan, no sales charge and no expense and general management fee, and no timing fee. Costs are $10,000 for the transaction commissions and a $5,000 annual investment management fee. The broker will advise if you need insurance, legal, and accounting service at no charge, other than their respective fees. Periodic status reports, reviews, and consultations are provided at no charge. If you decide not to go with the recommendations, you are not charged and you have no obligation. And here you have approximate fees of $15,000 or about 3 percent for the year. That's quite a savings over the financial planner's fees of close to $60,000 for the same work.

This example is an excessively bad or worse case scenario to show how abusive the costs can become and still be legal. Obviously, the industry boasts of financial planners who work diligently for their clients and keep costs down. I recommend you seek them out carefully.

The full-service stockbroker's role is changing. More and more brokers are working with larger sums of money—lump-sum distribution from insurance settlements, retirement plans, and inheritances. As I pointed out earlier, the trend is for full-service brokerage to work more frequently with outside investment advisors (money managers) and have the portfolio professionally managed. These brokers are called investment management consultants and are considered the talent scouts of the securities industry. They search for the best talent for your money.

"More and more brokers are working with larger sums of money."

You can compare the investment management consultant (broker) to an architect. Would you hire a contractor to build your medical building without first asking an architect to determine your needs? Of course you wouldn't. The architect would design a building that fit those needs and help hire a contractor to erect the building. The architect would then ride herd on the contractor to make sure he followed the blueprints. That's in essence what an investment management consultant does for you and your money—evaluates who the best manager would be to protect and increase your capital, and to monitor the performance so you get the most for your investment.

If you wanted a money manager to handle your portfolio, you would have to sift through over 9,000 advisors registered with the SEC to find the best one for you. I say too many investors spend more time picking out a mechanic to fix their auto than choosing a money manager to protect their financial future. Unless you were an expert mechanic, you wouldn't attempt to repair a blown engine. Why then would you attempt to do this with your hard earned investment funds?

The investment management consultant oversees your investments by monitoring the investment advisor's performance. This is perhaps the most important service offered. A good consultant will look for a long-term investment performance over five to ten years. Most are not interested in records that are up 80 percent one year, then down 40 percent the next. If you think about it you may not react to a stock in your portfolio moving from $20 to $18, but make it $200,00 to $180,000 and suddenly a lifetime of savings is under siege. That's where the watchful eye of the investment management consultant is critical, and this is what you are paying for.

Here's an example of what I'm getting at. In the February 1990 issue of *Forbes,* Mark Hulbert, editor of *Hulbert Financial Digest* and author of *The Hulbert Guide to Financial Newsletters* (Minerva Books) made a hard-hitting point about short-term results. He mentioned that at the top of the stock market hit parade in 1989 was Joe Granville's *Granville Market Letter.* Granville finished in first place with an average gain in his two portfolios of 368 percent, versus the S&P 500's 31.6 percent. But in the coverage the financial press gave Granville that year, it is rarely noted that his first-place showing could be traced to a 1,198 percent gain in his options portfolio—and that this same portfolio lost virtually everything in the previous four years. Mr. Hulbert says in his *Forbes* article that he can't imagine a much better illustration of the folly of focusing exclusively on one-year results. "A hypothetical $100,000 invested according to Granville's options recommendations on January 1, 1985 would have shrunk to just $3.77 by the end of 1988," says Mr. Hulbert. "Even after taking the huge 1989 gain into account, this portfolio would be worth only $48.94 today. What would be left of your $100,000 wouldn't buy a meal for two at a fine restaurant."

If you think about it, all of the Fortune 500 companies have professional money managers watching over their pension money. Why shouldn't you have someone just as talented to protect *your* life savings?

Time to Choose

By now, you probably have a pretty good idea of the various services a financial planner, a stockbroker/investment management consultant, and a money manager can provide. If you are an investor with an average income and under $100,000 to invest, more than likely you will choose either a planner or a stockbroker to help you choose a mutual fund, a tax-advantaged investment, or a stock portfolio. Or maybe you have decided to go it alone and buy CDs at your bank and some stocks at a good discount brokerage house and a good insurance policy. But, if you are a high-income earner, have some special tax problems, or a lump-sum distribution, the next chapter on professional investment management will be of particular interest to you. Either way, professional managers will, in the very least, educate the novice as well as the veteran investors, and help them to enjoy a lifetime of enlightened and intelligent financial management.

Professional investment advisors are, in my opinion, the wizards of Wall Street. For example, Warren Buffet is one of today's all-time great Hall-of-Fame-type investors. His mentor and teacher, Benjamin Graham, the most successful value investor of our century, told Warren a story that he likes to pass on:

"Mr. Market is your business partner, appearing daily, offering to buy and sell your interest in the business. Even though the business is stable, Mr. Market is anything but stable. At times he's euphoric and sees nothing but good aspects for the business and he'll buy at any price and all that he can. Then, he can get moody and depressed and see nothing but trouble ahead. On these occasions, he'll sell all he can at any price, unloading it on to others. One other emotional characteristic occurs when he is ignored. If he is trying to sell, you may decide not to buy. He'll then get depressed and you can make a better buy at a lower price. But, like Cinderella at the ball, you must heed one warning, or everything will turn into pumpkins and mice; Mr. Market is there to serve you, not to guide you. It is his pocketbook,

> **" Professional investment advisors are, in my opinion, the wizards of Wall Street."**

not his wisdom that you will find useful. If he shows up some day in a particularly foolish mood, you are free to either ignore him or to take advantage of him, but it will be disastrous if you fall under his influence. Indeed, if you aren't certain that you understand and can value your business far better than Mr. Market, you don't belong in the game. As they say in poker, 'If you've been in the game thirty minutes and you don't know who the patsy is, you're the patsy.'"

The last sentence of the story makes me shiver. If I were in that poker game, a feeling of fear would come over me, I'm sure, possibly damaging my ego and my wallet. I wouldn't join the game unless I had a good feeling about it. Yet, another successful money manager, Peter Lynch, points out that it is exactly that "wait and see" hesitation that is unnecessary, costly and outright foolish. Here's a quote from Mr. Lynch about people who wait for the Dow to break 3800 before they buy stocks: "That's like seeing a house you like that sells for $100,000 and waiting for it to reach $150,000 before buying it."

Peter Lynch started his famous mutual fund in 1977 and retired in 1990. A $100,000 investment in the Dow in 1977 would be worth $560,000 today. If one invested with Mr. Lynch over the same period, the $100,000 would have grown to a whopping $2,700,000.

Another master worth mentioning is Roger Engemann, president of Roger Engemann and Associates in Pasadena, California. While the Dow accumulated 856 percent from 1970 to 1990, Roger has accumulated 3,070 percent. High performance needs no excuses. Here is one of Roger's explanations on how he has mastered the art of investing:

"My feeling is that this is a great opportunity to invest in stocks. In the past, you've never gone wrong investing in stocks. So, when little dips come along in the market and Chicken Little jumps out of the coop telling you it's doomsday, don't believe it; it's nonsense. If you do anything during those periods, think of them as opportunities to invest more money. The future's going to be fantastic."

Listen to these masters and heed their advice, for they are truly the wizards of Wall Street.

9

The Investment Management System: Off to See the Wizard

Before I put the cart before the horse and begin describing investment management systems, I want you to take a good, hard look at your investment capital. Now, let's stop here for a moment because I've just said the key word: investment capital.

The definition of the term investment capital is *not* how much money you have left over at the end of the month. It's *not* how much you have accumulated in your savings account. And it's *not* the cash you were going to spend on your new home or life insurance policy. Investment capital is the money you NEVER HAVE TO TOUCH while you have income. An economic rule of thumb is to always have a cash reserve in your savings account equal to at least six months of your current salary. (Depending on the state of the economy, you may want to have a year's worth.) Experts say that this sum

> **"More and more individuals are becoming aware of the need for professional money management."**

should carry you over in case you have a career change, an emergency in the family, or some other type of unexpected financial burden. This rule of thumb applies to investment capital as well. Any cash over and above the six months (or one year) of cash reserve could be used as your investment capital. It is my opinion, and the opinion of other financial experts, that as long as your mortgage, life insurance, education, savings, and basic needs of food and clothing are fully covered, then you are ready to start talking "investment capital and investment management."

Now, back to what investment management is all about. Investment management is simply a system that helps you invest your capital. The individual managing the investment becomes the most critical ingredient and can make or break your portfolio. So, you have to decide for yourself: Are you going to manage your own investments or will you have someone else do it for you? You have three options: Choosing either a mutual fund, an independent investment advisor, or trying your own hand at it. Either way, a system must be used. I can't stress this enough. Using a systematic approach is the secret for accumulating wealth and the most profound, tried-and-true method for successful investing.

Don't try to manage your capital yourself unless you are an expert at it. I compare managing your own capital to flying an airplane if you've never flown one before. Or performing a delicate operation if you've never performed one before. Unless you are educated and experienced in the field, don't try it yourself—it could lead to disaster. So, if you have enough capital, say, at least $100,000, you can afford to hire your own pilot to fly your airplane.

This brings us to the dollar amount of cash you have on hand. Now, the size of your capital is very important when making the decision to choose an independent manager. Categorically, you are either in the "under $100,000 group" or the "over $100,000 group." If you are in the under $100,000 group, mutual funds will manage your funds for you for as low as a $50 per month investment. Mutual funds are an excellent system for accumulating wealth, and there are numerous books on how to evaluate and choose the one for you. If you are in the over $100,000 group, this next section is for you.

An Investment Management Evolution

Many of the brilliant investment managers who have guided billions of dollars in pension funds have broken away from their Fortune 500 companies to start their own smaller companies. They have seen the need for the smaller individual investor to have the same kind of investment guidance and management that is available to the corporate giants. A trend is starting to develop. More and more individuals are becoming aware of the need for professional money management as the world of stocks grows more complicated, more global. Stockbrokers, portfolio managers, and other professionals who watch the market carefully could not begin to keep an eye on all the various markets 24 hours a day, even with the easy access of computerization. So the trend is, simply, that in 10 years or less, all serious money management will be done by mutual funds or individual investment advisors.

The number one driving force behind the trend is the economics of compensation in this business. For those who can pick stocks, it will be more lucrative to be independent advisors. And if the stockbroker represents the advisor on behalf of the client, much of the compensation conflict of interest will be eliminated. The integrity of the relationship will be preserved. The performance results that clients want most from investment management can be obtained in this manner, be they from a mutual fund on a smaller investment capital scale or an individual manager on a larger scale.

What You Can Expect

Let me take you through a typical scene when I meet with a $100,000 investor. The first thing I like to do—and most financial experts will always do—is go through the financial planning exercise. I call it a "workup." In the workup, I assess the investable data by examining the primary documents I referred to earlier: the tax return, financial statement, and corporate data. The workup can include the estate if it is large enough, the will and the life insurance for estate tax planning. After the process is complete, I then identify what I refer to as "pockets of money," or money that is available to invest.

If the client has over $100,000, I discuss the option of using investment managers and explain that from this point on virtually the entire universe of managers is open to them. And from this universe, I will evaluate, select and monitor the performance of the money manager I feel will do the best job for her. That's what my client pays for. This is what is referred to in our business as "investment management consulting."

Over the years, I have developed an investment policy I firmly believe in—and many other brokers have done the same. The advisors that I choose to manage my clients' money all fit within the framework of my policy. Unfortunately, it has been a tradition in our industry to sell the customer whatever he wants, or to try to sell something that is popular, or that the firm is promoting. I have a big problem with that. I don't compromise my beliefs just to make a sale. Some of my competitors will try to get a sense of what kind of investments a prospect or client feels comfortable with and sell the heck out of it. This is what I call the "pressing your button" sale. To me it's not what the customer likes, but what the customer likes that I have access to that I can evaluate, then let them know if I like it as well. If a doctor was preparing to operate on you and started asking you questions like what kinds of instruments to use and what kinds of anesthesia to use, what would you do? I know what I would do—get off of the operating table and run like crazy! Guard your money as you would guard your life.

Protect Your Money of a Lifetime

Many of my clients are either saving for retirement, have sold a business, or have inherited a large sum of money. These individuals all have something in common. And that is, their money is irreplaceable and very dear to them. It's what I refer to as lifetime deposits, or money for a lifetime. Actually, all investors, in my opinion, have the same objectives. They may describe them in different terms but they all want: 1) to preserve capital, 2) maximum return if possible and 3) to pay the least taxes as possible. What each does with his money is of an individual nature. For example, it could be a young man turning 21 and collecting a $100,000 inheritance or an elderly woman collecting $200,000 from her late husband's insurance policy. These people do not want to lose their money, and if they invest, they want a better return than what they might get from a CD. It's at this juncture that I explain to my client that an important objective is to look for *consistent* rates of return as opposed to *maximum* rates of return.

You see, most investment advisors prepare their own presentation and performance data. For example, one advisor's record shows he made 27 percent in 1976. In 1987, he's up 10 percent; in 1989, he's up 23 percent. He has a 22.8 percent compounded rate of return. For the first quarter he's up 14 percent. Very good, but it's wise to go back at least 10 years and study the consistency of the performance. Some advisors will have very bad years and others very good years, but what you want to watch out for is the advisor who only presents the good years. It's important to understand that a manager's key objective is to preserve capital and increase returns. For example, if you project a $100,000 investment out 10 years at 10 percent a year compounded, Table 9-1 shows how it looks.

Table 9-1

End of	
Year 1	$110,000
Year 2	$121,000
Year 3	$133,100
Year 4	$146,410
Year 5	$161,051
Year 6	$177,156.
Year 7	$194,872
Year 8	$214,359
Year 9	$235,795
Year 10	$259,374

Your profit of $159, 374 (after you subtract your initial $100,000 capital investment) nets you a compounded annual rate of return per year of 15.9 percent.

This is an important distinction. I highlight this fact to my clients because human nature being what it is, most people pick the manager who shows the highest figure for the year. But the smart thing is to look at the lower end of the scale—say 10 percent per year for three years—because with compounding added in, you are actually receiving 15 percent per year as shown above.

Obviously, managers cringe when investors look only at the bad years because that gives you a jaded view of their performance. But you can look at benchmark years like 1987 and 1990—two very bad years for the market—and if the manager was able to preserve capital and do as well or better than the S&P during those tough times, then I'd say you have a good manager on your side. Especially in comparison to other managers and other investment vehicles during the same time period.

Here's another way to look at it. I never tell my clients they will never have a losing year. That would be preposterous. But, if you temper your low years with your winning years, your average should be better than you would have received in a CD! For example, if you factor in the 23.9 percent return you received in 1989 with the –4 percent in 1990, you would be receiving approximately 10 percent per year.

The Pot of Gold Is Achieved through Consistent Performance

As I mentioned earlier in the book, it is impossible to predict with any accuracy which advisors are going to do well in the future. My "Rainbow Effect" theory applies here and is worth stressing again. We all can see a rainbow, we all know where it's located, but no one can ever tell us where it's going to appear next. The rainbow theory teaches that it is totally unrealistic to presume which investment advisor will be the best performer over the coming six to twelve months.

What you need to understand about this business is that advisors run hot and cold. If you're going to play the derby (not do performance research or work with a broker/consultant) and you're going to give Advisor A $500,000 and Advisor B $500,000 and wait and see which advisor has the better performance over a one-year period, you could easily wind up doing business with the worse of the two, just because the better advisor had a down year during that period among many good years, and the advisor with a worse performance over the long haul just happened to have a really hot year during the period of your investment. Sound confusing? Just look for consistency—and look for it over a five- to ten-year time period. It's pretty easy to get frustrated with the so-called investment guru if you're only making 2-3 percent a year for three or four years in a row when the year before you invested your money he was famous for making a blazing 80 percent return!

Forget about the advisor who puts half your money in utilities and half in gold, betting on a collapse of the economic system—that interest rates dive and the dollar fails. Obviously, if that occurs and if both utilities and gold rise, he's the star performer. The rainbow has fortunately fallen on top of that advisor.

Bulls, Bears, Diesels and Airplanes

I would be willing to bet my career on the fact that most people are happy with a rate of return slightly better than that of a CD. And I say to my clients, that if I can't do better than a CD, then you don't need me. Obviously, there's no doubt in my mind that their portfolio will do well, but, I'm not promising to beat the Dow Jones average. For example, the accounts of one excellent investment advisor I follow closely were up 24 percent in 1985 while the Dow was up 31 percent. Does that mean my advisor failed? Not at all. My objective is not to beat the Dow. My objective is to preserve capital and receive a rate of return better than that of CDs.

You may think this is too conservative. Well, let me make an analogy. I'll call it the Diesel Engine Approach. Here you are driving along in your car with a slow, but strong diesel engine under the hood. You look around and notice all the fast sports cars passing you by, especially that beautiful Ferrari. But give that diesel engine enough highway and no time constraints, and you'll leave that Ferrari in the dust.

Now, as an investor, a certain personal responsibility comes with managing your money. You must become knowledgeable in certain aspects of investment management—your money of a lifetime is at stake. Let's take another look at that pilot analogy. If you have never flown in an airplane and suddenly the plane flies through an air pocket and experiences turbulence, you might have a cardiac arrest thinking you're about to fall to the earth right then and there. However, if you had some basic understanding of the airplane and its operation, you'd know it's normal to hit air pockets and would stop thinking about bailing out. It just takes a fair amount of education before you learn to feel comfortable with the ride.

Once you feel comfortable, many new worlds of investing will be open to you. You'll be able to make informed decisions and you'll enjoy working with your broker and your money manager. So, let me continue discussing the various aspects of investment management I feel you should be aware of before handing over your money of a lifetime.

You Don't Need 3-D Glasses for This System

I happen to love teaching and so it gives me a thrill to explain the dynamics of the investment management system that I and all of my investment advisors use—the D3 System: Diversification, Diversification, Diversification. Diversification techniques remind me of the strategies used by the general in charge of the battle. When fighting a battle and it's going well, your troops have the enemy on a rout and you really have a rally going. Then you can afford to either let all the troops continue battling or start bringing them back in reserves, re-establishing the ground you've gained.

When the battle goes poorly and the enemy has busted through, you now implement your reserves. It's much the same in the world of investments. It's all tactical, not emotional.

The first level of the D3 system is D1. This level helps us determine how much to invest in stocks, cash equivalents, or cash reserves. A portfolio manager may like the market for an entry point and invest 60 percent of the funds, leaving 40 percent in cash equivalents. This way, the manager can use the cash and take advantage of buying during a down market.

> **″ Forget about the advisor who puts half your money in utilities and half in gold, betting on a collapse of the economic system.″**

Many times, at this first level, some managers will add bonds to their diversification. This is called a "balanced" portfolio, but as you know by now, I prefer not to use any system that incorporates bonds. However, I must point out that there are exceptions to all rules and this includes my rule of never buying bonds. I do work with two investment advisors who manage bonds in a balanced portfolio for a few select clients of mine. The few sophisticated clients I am referring to understand thoroughly that bonds are to be managed with equal, if not more, attention than is given to stocks. When you take a position in bonds, you do so by knowing when to get out and when to get back in. In other words, the manager has an upside and a downside target that he sticks to, and the bonds are managed like any other diversified position in the portfolio.

This policy differs from mainstream thinking. It is not acceptable, in my opinion, to simply "park" bonds in a portfolio and call it diversified. This is an excuse to help a broker make a sale. It does nothing to enhance performance. In fact, it's a liability for long-term performance! On the other hand, if the advisor uses bonds as just one more tool for diversification in investment positioning, this is accept-

> **t is not acceptable, in my opinion, to simply "park" bonds in a portfolio and call it diversified."**

able. All in all, both parties need to be fairly sophisticated and understand the nature of bonds and how they react to the market and to the economy.

D2 level of the diversification system is: Don't put all your eggs in one basket. In my opinion, a good manager will establish a diversified portfolio by purchasing the initial portfolio of stocks in 5 to 10 percent increments. You see, you really want to own enough shares of a stock so that if it does well, it contributes to the success of the portfolio. That's why you want to keep positioning the stock at around the 3-5 percent level. If you're buying 1 or 2 percent of a certain stock and you've done ingenious homework and it's tripled, you're not doing a whole lot for the bottom line. You want your work to pay off. The opposite is also true—you don't want to own too much of any one stock. Let's look at a typical scenario. You own 10 percent of a stock you really like and the price, let's say, doubles and now represents 20 percent of your entire portfolio. OK, then your manager sells half and you complain. Why did you sell it? I thought you liked it. Why not keep all of it and watch it continue to rise? What's going on here?

Well, I'll tell you what's going on. Had the manager kept all of it, it would have amounted to irresponsible port-folio management. What if, the next day, you heard on the radio that some kook put arsenic in the water of the big soft drink company you held a 20 percent position in? That's right—your account takes a nose-dive and you're left hold-ing the bag and your advisor takes the heat.

The third level of the D3 system is diversification by industry group. Here we take a look at industries that, through research, we feel have the best potential of strong earnings growth. We then invest in the company stock of those industries and, as a result, own a layer of quality stocks within a layer of quality industries, and have further safely diversified the portfolio. Obviously, what separates the am-ateurs from the pros in the investment management busi-ness is the ability to predict with improving odds which segment of the economy will prosper in the ensuing months. And that's what you are paying for. The D3 system is the most efficient means of diversification I know that does not lead to redundancy in a portfolio.

Integrity of Compensation

My favorite part of the explanation of managed money is the compensation arrangement. It has what I call an inherent integrity of structure. The broker/consultant, client and in-vestment advisor are all motivated to focus on performance with this method. And here's why.

As a generally accepted standard, the investment advisor accepts a 1 percent fee each year on the balance of the portfolio. This fee is calculated on the dollar amount of assets under management. So, on a typical $100,000 under management, an investor would pay $1,000 a year. The advisors place orders to buy and sell securities based on their management style, which could be either domestic or global, to name two specific styles. Now, the commissions generated by this trading activity do not flow to them, but instead they flow to the broker who referred the client. This is a very important point to underscore here because it is critical that the individual making the buy or sell decisions should not be the person receiving the commissions.

Let me regress for a moment. There was a point in my career where I was making what we call "position trades." I could take a look at my position book, and depending upon what mood I was in (or how much money I needed) I would think, "Gosh, I could figure out a good reason to sell this stock and make a big commission today." It was really a double-edged sword because sometimes a stock was in trouble, but I didn't want to sell because I knew I would make a large commission and in addition to losing money on the performance of the stock, I would look bad because I was taking such a big commission on the sell side. Next thing you know, the stock continued to drop and because I was so worried about how I would appear to my customer if I had sold earlier, I created even more losses for my client. The standard "position" broker is a self-defeating spot to be in. It can really create a dilemma. So the broker knows it is in his best interest to allow the investment advisor to make the trading decisions.

A fine, long time client provided me with some historical data that I think is typical and represents what to expect from this style of investing. The client started his investment program in 1985 with a $600,000 account on deposit. The percent commissions and trades per year are shown in Figure 9-2.

Collectively, the commissions averaged 1.90 percent of capital on deposit. The 1988 commissions were low because there were few reasons to change the portfolio. 1989 commissions were high due to not only a change in market conditions, but also to a change of money mangers as we shifted from Manager A to Manager B. In bull markets (1989) we tend to hold positions and ride them all the way up and the commission activity comes to a standstill. To recover from the crash, we had to keep the stock we owned—because anything after October 1987 rose. However, you'll notice that in years like 1987 where we have catastrophic events, you'll see a dramatic increase in commission activity.

I always emphasize to my advisors to keep trades of stocks to a minimum. This keeps your costs down and boosts performance. Performance increases value and managers are paid to create value. Clients are satisfied with increased value from increased performance. And so it goes.

As a consequence of caring about my client's performance, I get referrals and added deposits. This, in turn, increases my commissions. Like everyone else, I like having more money, but receiving it as a result of taking good care of my clients is a great feeling.

Figure 9-2

1985—1.28% and 20 trades
1986—2.11% and 24 trades
1987—2.19% and 27 trades
1988—0.5% and 10 trades
1989—3.40% and 63 trades

Ethics and Integrity Win Hands Down

This structure is the best way to manage investments as it both emphasizes integrity and eliminates the conflict of interest. The advisors do not share in the commissions, therefore they have no incentive to "churn" the accounts. To the contrary, any excess trading increases commission costs, thereby reducing value as well as reducing the fees of the advisors. And we, the brokers receiving the commissions, cannot influence changes to the portfolio. Actually, it is considered to be inside information if, for example, I found out that one of the advisors was selling 80,000 shares of XYZ Corp. and I bought "puts" (an option trading strategy) on the XYZ Corp. stock and profited from the knowledge that my advisor was selling the stock. This is called front-running by the SEC, and is considered illegal.

"Keep trades of stocks to a minimum."

My investment philosophy is that if I give my clients a product or service they are happy and satisfied with, they will stay with me. And if I'm lucky, I'll get a referral or two from each client. This way, my business will double, triple, and so on. To look at the financial side, I'll share some numbers with you to illustrate how successful my techniques have been. When I began my investment consulting business in 1981, I gathered $10 million under management and I received about 2 percent a year gross commission revenue on that amount. I wasn't making the 6 or 8 percent at a time up front that could have been made on other investment products. Today, I have under management over $200 million in deposits. And I'm proud to say I still have the accounts that gave me the first $10 million over 10 years ago.

You see, investment management is not a complicated process; it's not frightening. What is frightening is turning over your money of a lifetime to someone who doesn't use a system or who gambles away your capital.

10

A Few Last Words Worth Repeating: Continuing Education

We've finally arrived at that part of the book where you're probably asking the questions, "OK, now what? Am I going to be left hanging, wondering what to do next? I understand what it takes to be a successful conservative investor, but where do I go for help?" Those are valid questions and ones I'm often asked. That's why I've compiled a reference section at the end of this chapter recommending the best books, magazines, newspapers, newsletters, referral numbers, and money management firms to help get you started with your investing program.

But first, let me say a few important last words. You need to keep several facts in clear sight:

1. Human nature will always tear away at your investments if you don't have patience and a good accumulation system.

2. Remember the difference between investing and speculating.

3. Don't be greedy.

4. Before investing, make certain all your basic needs are provided for and that you have "extra" capital for your financial program.

5. If you decide not to handle your own investment portfolio, choose a broker or a money manager who uses a low-risk, long-term accumulation system that offers consistent performance over a five-year or longer period of time.

6. Continue to educate yourself.

The process of successful investing lies more within yourself than with all the investment experts. In your search for successful investment techniques you must understand that even vast sums of data can be rendered neutral if you don't understand the technicalities and subtleties of your own investment system. In simpler terms: Don't kid yourself *and* don't allow an investment salesperson to kid you.

So many people carry a false sense of security about their investment knowledge just because they watch some

Wall Street television show every week, or read the *Wall Street Journal* every day. As in life, the truly wise people recognize and accept their shortcomings and keep searching for the most successful way of planning their financial future.

I've often said my main stroke of genius was in recognizing how blind I was in 1980, and finally having the vision to see that the real pros in this business are managing large pools of capital. They're not selling products to individuals regardless of their worth or soundness, whether or not they are in the best interest of the client.

The Conservative Investor

Without exception, every investor I've had the good fortune to counsel has told me straight away that their investment style was conservative. Whether they are or not is debatable, however. My definition of a conservative investor is a person who recognizes his investing limitations and so chooses strategies he understands and is familiar with. This way, if his portfolio takes a dip, he understands why, and will exercise more patience and control than the average investor and will not be tempted to sell at the wrong time. It has been proven that the most important tool the true conservative investor has in his favor is time. In time, performance expectations are met and—presto!—successful investing is achieved. The conservative investor is a successful investor.

I'd also like to point out here that I don't consider the long-term holder of *bonds* to be a conservative investor. In the end, this investor's false sense of conservatism makes his portfolio a loser simply because he fails to accept the reality of inflation's effects on the bonds in the portfolio.

Accumulation System

By now, you understand the importance of an accumulation system: socking your capital away in an investment vehicle that you can't touch for a period of five years or longer—just long enough to show you how to weather stock market cycles and how compounding affects your principal investment. If you are trying to build a nest egg for your retirement, a mutual fund is an excellent vehicle for your capital. Better yet, look into a variable annuity which allows for the tax-deferred accumulation of growth stock mutual funds.

It is also very helpful to study stock market history—plus it's fascinating! The study of market historical cycles is a key to understanding your accumulation system. You will learn to appreciate down cycles because your system can capitalize on the temporary downturns as the market resumes its historic up movement. It's all very logical and systematic.

Money of a Lifetime

If you have already accumulated your "money of a lifetime" you can now begin searching for an investment management consultant who can assist you in selecting an investment advisor to manage and protect those assets. A special referral number is offered by The Institute of Investment Management Consultants in Phoenix, Arizona, and the Investment Management Consulting Association in Denver, Colorado, for those who need help in locating one in their city. (See reference section.)

Your money of a lifetime, as you remember, is the serious capital you have earned that will be needed to help support you and your family after your retirement. Four elements that you need to keep in mind before turning over your money of a lifetime are:

1. preserving your capital

2. maintaining earning power

3. paying little or no taxes

4. being happy by beating the CD and inflation rates.

Everybody and his brother are hanging "financial professional" shingles these days. Individuals outside of the securities industry are calling themselves financial professionals—some CPAs, insurance salespeople, attorneys. Granted, many of these individuals are very talented and will do their best for you. However, always know who you are dealing with. There are many unscrupulous people trying to take advantage of the unsuspecting investor. Just be sure to talk only to licensed, certified investment professionals.

> **"The process of successful investing lies more within yourself than with all the investment experts."**

According to statistics, many of you reading this book are at least 40-something (including me). And many of you are at a point where you will soon be blooming financially. You are entering your higher pay scale cycle and have coped with life's challenges such as your children's college tuitions costs, purchasing a home, buying a business, and so on. For the sake of retirement security, you have to make the correct decisions in the time you have left with the money power you possess.

Let's get some ground rules down and some misconceptions cleared up. It may help to photocopy these guidelines and put them in your financial folder.

1. Pay down debt. Pay off the 12 percent, 18 percent or higher credit card interest. Your money can't earn that on a guaranteed basis, so pay it off. You can't even deduct that interest on your taxes anymore.

2. Save money and build your liquidity by using any possible tax-deferred system such as pension accounts, 401Ks, IRAs, deferred annuities and/or variable annuities. Systematic savings that compound tax-free are the best net worth building accounts you can have.

3. Remember the human nature flaw. Don't give in to greed and impatience. Long-term investing will prove to be your most successful ally. Don't trade the market unless you are experienced at it. Use a system.

3a. Corollary to number 3. If you must trade the market, learn to buy in when it seems scary, like July of 1974, August of 1982 or October of 1987. Then when the market is wonderful, sell!

3b. Corollary to number 3a. When you have bought into what you think is a "buy" market and you are too early, don't lose your cool. It will recover and go to new highs. If you have bought quality stocks, they will follow the market.

4. Remember, every year will have its crisis in the media. We baby boomers have been through Tricky

Dick, Watergate, Vietnam, Credit Crunches, Oil Embargoes, and now Budget Deficits and Recession. In our lifetime, the Dow has gone from 565 to over 3000. Don't think today's crisis will hold the value of American stocks down. They have a natural historic evolution to trend upward. I believe we will live to see the Dow hit 10,000.

5. There is no historical data that demonstrate investing in bonds over the long term is a good investment. Avoid all bonds—tax-free, tax-exempt, corporates, and so on—unless you are a professional who trades or manages them as closely as stocks. In my opinion, bonds are bad.

6. Tax-deferred compounding accounts create more net after-tax income and are safer than tax-exempt securities.

7. Investigate and evaluate the investment management professional you choose to work with. Remember the best financial planning advice should cost the least.

8. To get rich for sure:

   a. Save money

   b. Don't lose money

   c. Do steps a) and b), otherwise endeavor to be a nationally-ranked expert in your field of expertise. Don't try to be lucky; that's up to fate, not you.

If you can do all of this, you're on your way to becoming a Streetwise Investor. Good luck!

REFERENCE SECTION

Money Managers

The following money managers are just a few of the many professionals who are available to you. I advise you to call or write them, requesting an information kit which will include performance, investment style and philosophy, account minimums, credentials of investment advisor(s), and other pertinent information.

> Beutel Goodman Capital Management LTD
> 2030 Texas-Commerce Tower
> Houston, TX 77002
> 713-221-1719

> Brandes Investment Management
> 12760 High Bluff Drive #160
> San Diego, CA 92130
> 1-800-237-7119

> Calamos Asset Management, Inc.
> 2001 Spring Road #750
> Oak Brook, IL 60591-9004
> 708-571-7115

> Roger Engemann & Assoc., Inc.
> 600 N. Rosemead Blvd.
> Pasadena, CA 91107-2101
> 818-351-9686

Investment Advisors, Inc.
1100 Louisiana #2600
Houston, TX 77002
713-659-2611

Investment Management Associates, Inc.
11 Greenway Plaza #710
Houston, TX 77046
713-850-0330

JMC Capital Management, Inc.
Two Lakeway Center #1400
3850 N. Causeway Blvd.
Metairie, LA 70002
504-833-1111

Kingston Financial Services, Inc.
M. King Grossman, President
2700 Post Oak Bend #1350
Houston, TX 77056
713-621-1155

NWQ Investment Management Co.
655 S. Hope St. 11th floor
Los Angeles, CA 90017
213-624-6700

OPCAP Investment Management Services
Frank Minard
OPCO Towers
3800 World Financial Center
New York, NY 10281
800-999-6726

Oppenheimer & Co., Inc.
Special Accounts Department
Stan Schwartz
333 Clay Street
Houston, TX 77020
1-800-999-6726

Princeton International
Bob Watson, President
12695 Whittington
Houston, TX 77077
713-584-9289

Starbuck, Tisdale & Assoc.
L. David Tisdale, President
301 E. Carillo St.
Santa Barbara, CA 93101
805-963-5963

Vaughan, Nelson, Scarborough & McConnel, Inc.
6300 Texas Commerce Tower
Houston, TX 77002-3071
713-224-2545

Widmann, Siff & Co., Inc.
#2 E. Montgomery Ave. #200
Ardmore, PA 19003
215-520-0500

Charles Fahy's Recommended "Investment Course"

Many of you might think you don't have the time or the
money to learn any more about investing (other than read-

ing this book!). Yet you realize that knowledge + using a system is the key to being successful at managing your own destiny over the monies you are concerned about. So, let me recommend an investment course you can take at your leisure for as low as $30 per year or as high as $150. This course will take you from the basic elementary level to the most sophisticated and successful aspects of investing.

Elementary School: Start with a one-year subscription to *Money* magazine. Read this publication until you are entirely familiar with all of its various departments and features. *Money* covers almost everything under the sun—from lottery ticket winners to truly conservative successful investing techniques.

High School: To continue expanding your educational horizon, move on to *Kiplinger's Personal Finance* (formerly *Changing Times*). With this subscription you will be exposed to a more serious format. The articles critique investments and introduce you to future trends in the business of forecasting. *Money* magazine is great if you want to learn what has already happened in the investment world; *Personal Finance* will predict what is likely to happen in its future.

College: You are now ready to add *Business Week* to your list of reading material. With it you will develop a sense of which companies are succeeding or failing in the various business trends and cycles. *Business Week* will also introduce you to some investment systems that are attempting to deal with these various trends and cycles.

Graduate School: At this graduate level you might want to take a double major since the next two publications take separate paths. *Fortune* magazine moves your education in the direction of the affairs of the corporate world. Here you will find corporate analysis which will cover a company's attempt to capture certain markets and cycles. You will join the club of CEOs, CFOs, and board chairpersons. You will understand the various stages of the investment cycles—i.e., start-ups; venture capital; initial public offerings (IPOs); young, emerging growth companies; and the vulnerable blue chips.

The other path is to be found in *Forbes* magazine. Here you truly enter the real world of investments. You will be exposed to the world of investment systems. You'll learn that to succeed as an investor, you need a proven investment system that has been proven historically. You'll learn about the investments that have succeeded or failed. *Forbes* is unique in its strength to expose the naked truth about investments. It pulls no punches. In my opinion, it has editorial integrity second to no other periodical on the subject of investment systems.

You are now ready to select your own path to successful investing. You can be a self-directed investor using investment tools such as no-load mutual funds, discount brokerages, or investment advisors. The other route you can take is to select a broker/investment management consultant who can provide both financial planning and an investment system for you.

Periodicals You Should Review for Consideration:

1. *The Wall Street Journal*

2. *Investor's Business Daily*

3. *Investor's Digest*

4. *The Hulbert Financial Digest*—This is a monitoring service that analyzes returns for the model portfolios of nearly 130 newsletters. The newsletter gives you a peek at their rankings for the past three, five, and

eight years. Hulbert also measures how much risk each adviser takes to achieve returns. This can help you decide whether you can stomach the gyrations a letter's recommended stocks might take. 703-683-5905

5. *Forbes*—This publication is a must for investment reading. Forbes has the cream of the crop investment writers who write objectively and critically on investments in general.

6. *Business Week*—Excellent reading that supplements what the daily papers miss on business, the economy, and investing.

7. *Money*—Probably has the best mixture of critical articles on financial planning, investing, and historical statistical data which provides a continuing source of information for investors.

8. *Fortune*—This magazine better serves those investors "doing it on their own." You'll receive in-depth analyses of particular companies and news of key investment industry professionals.

9. *Kiplinger's Personal Finance* (formerly *Changing Times*)—Vast array of continuing education and predictions of future trends in investing.

Books for Further Study for Graduate Students:

1. *Stocks, Bonds, Bills and Inflation - Historical Returns 1926-87*
   By Roger G. Ibbotson and Rex A. Sinquefield
   (Chicago: The Research Foundation of the Institute of Chartered Financial Analysts, 1991)

This is the statistical bible of the Wall Street historical track record. If you are the type that wants the raw facts to draw your own conclusions, this is a "must own" book. It compares the various investments over various periods of time. Its best value is in giving you the simple fact that stocks—left alone—out-perform all other investments. I've seen this to be true as I look back with 20/20 vision on 20 years of investing. If you are an investor, this is must reading.

2. *The First-Time Investor - Start Out Safe and Smart*
   by Larry Chambers and Kenn Miller
   (Chicago: Probus Publishing Co., 1991)

Chambers provides objective, clear insight to the new investor. He was a successful broker and now consults to the securities industry. Very well-written in easy-to-understand language.

3. *The Prudent Investor. The Definitive Guide to Professional Investment*
   by James P. Owen
   (Chicago: Probus Publishing Co., 1990)

This text is written by a successful former broker who is a co-founder of the Investment Management Consultants Association and is now a managing director of NWQ Investment Management Co. It covers investment management from A to Z.

4. *Up on the Market with Carter Randall*
   As told to William J. Gianopulos
   (Chicago: Probus Publishing Co., 1992)

Mr. Randall, co-host of the "Wall Street Week" television show with Louis Rukeyser, rose through the bank trust department ranks. His book's insight into stocks and bonds is similar in content to *Streetwise Investor*, but written outside of the Wall Street boundaries. Full of straight talk and solid advice.

5. *Investing in Convertible Securities. Your Complete Guide to the Risks and Rewards.*
   by John P. Calamos
   (Chicago: Dearborn, 1990)

Former B52 Bombardier who strategically calculated surface to air missiles in Vietnam during the war. He seems to apply the same careful strategies to convertible securities to make for a winning portfolio.

6. *Value Investing Today*
   by Charles H. Brandes
   (Chicago: Richard D. Irwin, 1990)

One of the current deans of global investing, Mr. Brandes finds value companies by searching the world over. He is a faithful follower of the late Benjamin Graham and consistently one of the best performing money managers in the U.S.

7. *The New Contrarian Investing Strategy*
   by David Dreman
   (New York: Random House, 1992)

Important psychological aspects of successful investing are used by going against the market. Being a contrarian can help you find good value in the marketplace, if you practice patience and study Mr. Dreman's ad-

vice. Mr. Dreman is a regular *Forbes* magazine columnist and his wisdom should be followed carefully.

8. *Master Your Stockbroker*
   by Patrick G. Finegan, Jr. Esq.
   (The Palindrome Press)

This is a wise book for either novice or seasoned investor. It contains many of the secrets you need to know
about working with stockbrokers and financial planners. Even though I consider it a "bitch book," it has
some good insight.

9. *Asset Allocation*
   by Roger C. Gibson
   (Chicago: Richard D. Irwin, 1991)

A valuable book which discusses in-depth methods of
investment systems and strategies that have withstood
the test of time.

10. *Reminiscences of a Stock Operator*
    by Edwin LeFevre
    (New York: Traders Press, Inc.)

This is an all-time classic offering fundamental insight
into the securities trade. Yet, it wisely explains how the
main character plays against public greed. It reflects
the survivor's instinct of a trader. It was written as a
novel, but is in fact, based on the life of the famous Jesse
Livermore, who was known for his shorting the 1929
stock market. He died penniless.

11. *One Up on Wall Street*
    by Peter Lynch
    (New York: Simon & Schuster)

Peter Lynch is a living Wall Street legend as well as a household name in investing. His book is brilliantly simple in its explanation of how stocks work.

12. *Hulbert Guide to Financial Newsletters*
    Mark Hulbert
    (Alexandria, VA: Minerva Books, 1989)

Provides investors with clear and objective evaluations of over 100 investment newsletters. Each publication is described in detail, noting methods and philosophies.

Institutions and Organizations to Help You Locate Money Managers and Obtain Investment Research Material

1. The Institute for Econometric Research
   3471 N. Federal Highway
   Ft. Lauderdale, FL 33306
   800-442-9000

2. Institute for Investment Management Consultants
   3101 N. Central Ave. #560
   Phoenix, AZ 85012
   602-265-6114

3. Investment Management Consultants Association
   9101 E. Kenyon Ave. #3000
   Denver, CO 80237
   303-770-3377

Investment Newsletters

1. Dick Davis Digest
   Box 8547
   Fort Lauderdale, FL 33310
   (305) 771-7111

2. Market Logic
   Institute for Economic Research
   3471 N. Federal Hwy.
   Fort Lauderdale, FL 33306-1019
   (305) 563-9000

3. Forecast & Strategies
   Phillips Publishing Inc.
   7811 Montrose Rd.
   Potomac, MD 20854
   (301) 424-3700

4. Wall St. Digest Inc.
   One Sarasota Towers
   Sarasota, FL 34236
   (813) 854-5500

Index

L
Lawsuit, 29
 see Investor
Leverage/leveraging, 72, 79, 131
Liabilities, 141
Life insurance, 149
 see Single
Limited partnership, 13, 142, 148
Liquidity factor, 73
Loss, 86
 see Capital
Lump sum, 127
 distribution, 20, 21, 152
Lynch, Peter, 54, 154

M
Management, 84
 see Capital, Investment, Money,
  Portfolio
 fees, 142, 144
Market
 see Bond, Stock
 cycle(s), 36, 92
 investment returns, 44
 risk, 46
 value, 77
Maturity, 48, 81, 128
Merrill Lynch, 3
Money
 (magazine), 33, 134
 managers, 20, 144, 151, 152, 158,
  174
  list, 180-182, 189-190
 management, 16, 22
 firms, 174
 protection, 160-162
Mortgage, 65
 see Federal, Veterans
 instruments, 46
Municipal(s), 42, 49
 see National

bond trust, 88
Utility District bonds (M.U.D.s),
 60
Mutual fund, 42, 60, 95, 96, 131,
 144, 145, 146, 148, 149, 152,
 157, 176
 see Bond, Growth

N
National Mutual Fund Shares, 61
National Trust Tax-Exempts, 68
Net Asset Value (NAV), 50, 71,
 72, 79, 85
New York Stock Exchange
 (NYSE), 73
North American Securities Ad-
 ministrators Association, 144
Nuveen, John & Co., 88

O
Open-end fund, 17
Option(s), 79
 see Stock
 portfolio, 151
Option-writing techniques, 44

P
Package bonds, 17, 88
Partnership, 14
 see Limited
 award program, 18
Passbook rate, 129
Pension, 125, 126
 account, 27
 fund, 141
 plan, 123
Performance, 9, 33, 42, 45, 54, 63,
 70, 72, 77, 145, 148, 150, 160,
 162-163, 167, 169, 174
 see Portfolio, Stock
 charts, 53